PIPERS HILL

PIPERS HILL

Memories of a Country Childhood

by *Oliver Holt*

with illustrations by the author

O joy! that in our embers
Is something that doth live,
That nature yet remembers
What was so fugitive!

MARSTON HOUSE

Published in 1992 by Marston House,
Marston Magna, Yeovil, Somerset BA22 8DH
Designed and produced by Alphabet & Image Ltd,
Sherborne, Dorset DT9 3LU

ISBN 0 9517700 2 0

A CIP catalogue record for this book
is available from the British Library.

Typeset by Kendalls, Milborne Port, Dorset

Printed by Remous Printers, Milborne Port, Dorset

CONTENTS

To my wife

FOREWORD

The following chapters have been written at intervals during quite a long period. Some of them are based on articles which, to my delight and gratification, were thought good enough to be printed in *The Times, Country Life,* the *Western Gazette* and the late lamented *Blackwood's Magazine.* I am very grateful to the Editors of those papers for the pleasure and encouragement they gave me by accepting my offerings and for giving permission for them to be reprinted here.

But when, not so long ago, I had the idea of collecting and adding to them, I was at a loss to think of a way of giving them some measure of coherence and unity. It came to me one day that I might do this by relating them to my childhood, when in the delightful home not far from London – Blake speaks of a 'pleasant Surrey Bower' – in which I was so fortunate as to be born and brought up, my love of Natural History – such a solemn term I always feel – was itself born and fostered.

In acting on this idea I have revised and altered, in some cases beyond recognition, the original pieces and added some that are new. Well aware of the slightness of their content, I thought, no doubt presumptuously, that further coherence and even a little weight might be added if I illustrated them with my own drawings, especially as the making of drawings has been a life-long pastime and a means by which I have tried to express my thanks for the gift of life and my praise of the Creator: again I fear I speak with too much confidence.

It will soon be apparent to any reader who has some knowledge of birds and the other creatures I have been writing about that I have nothing to tell him that he does not already know. The most I can hope for is that I may convey to him some of the pleasure I have derived from my study of them and, now and then, by showing how some aspect of their beauty and individuality has appealed to me, add to his own admiration and delight.

I should like also to feel that I have shewn what treasure may be laid up for the young if encouraged in their early years to open their eyes and ears to the beauty of the natural world around them.

I wrote just now of my fortunate childhood. To that piece of good fortune another almost as great was granted me: my love of birds and flowers and butterflies was immensely enlarged and encouraged by the Headmaster of my preparatory school, Littleton Powys. To him, therefore, as to my parents, I owe a deep and recurring debt of gratitude.

THE SNIPE ARE DRUMMING

ne of us would come running in from the lawn on a hazy March morning. 'Mother, where are you? Come quickly!' My mother would call back in alarm from her desk, picturing a broken bone or bleeding flesh: 'I'm here, in the drawingroom; whatever's the matter?'

'Quick! You must come. The snipe are drumming!'

Report of an accident could not have brought her more quickly to her feet and out she hurried into the mist. 'How lovely! But did you really hear one? Surely it's too early. I expect you were imagining it.'

'Oh, no; we all heard it. Listen!'

The garden was silent and still, the mist wrapped close about it like a sheet drawn over a sleeping figure. No breath of wind stirred the muffled branches. Sound and movement came only when a saturated leaf or twig brimmed over and let fall a drop of moisture with a light pit-pat.

'That always happens,' would be the complaint. 'Just when you specially want something to do what it's supposed to, it never does.'

Looking upward we could see that the grey of the enveloping gauze became silvery and then almost golden the higher it spread, until right above us there appeared an unmistakable saucer of palest blue. 'It's going to be fine. The sun can't be far off.' And there, suddenly, it was, a sixpence spinning behind the frayed edges of the mist. It was certainly a typical 'snipe' morning.

'Hark!' An expectant pause.

'That was a motor-bike, stupid.'

'No it wasn't, I'm positive!'

'Someone will have to run in and get me a coat,' my mother said, 'I'm chilly. And I can't wait long; I've lots of letters to write.' Someone ran.

The garden sloped down to water-meadows, the boundary between them being a shallow stream, known to us as the Ditch to distinguish it from a slightly broader water-course called the Bourne, which received its meagre tribute at the furthest corner of the garden and went on to join the River a few hundred yards away. Along the Ditch grew willows, which smouldered with a deeper glow as the mist lightened, and alders with catkins of bronze.

Bribed by her coat for a longer stay out of doors, my mother began to look about to see how the daffodils and other spring flowers were coming up. Such inspections were wont to arouse in her a nice blend of disappointment and satisfaction. 'There are very few angel's tears this year; but look at those dog's tooth violets! I don't remember them growing there before.' We gathered round to examine their pensive rosy heads and smooth leaves mottled like a snake's skin. So intent were we that we missed the start of the commotion above us. We had been taken unawares and were already in the midst of an increasingly voluminous hum. A snipe was 'drumming' indeed. For a few moments the whole garden seemed to vibrate with the penetrating murmur. It stopped with a sudden whiz; and when silence and steadiness returned it was hard to believe that the sound had come from outside – that it had not been a spasm of one's own body.

'There, Mother, now do you believe us?' She was of course delighted. It was one of the sounds she loved best in the whole year. She declared that Spring began the moment she first heard it.

The sun, now an angel with a flaming sword, was driving the mist from the garden. Shadows of bushes and trees were laid down and beyond their prostrate shapes the crystals of dew were licked up as soon as they began to sparkle. On all sides the crocus candles took the wandering flame and the blossom shone on prunus and almond.

We had not to wait long for the next snipe. Soon the strange vibration began to emerge from the silent sky, distant at first, but swiftly growing in volume until it drove into the 'deep heart's core'. Almost all writers about birds, not excepting T.A. Coward and Lord Grey, say that a snipe 'bleats'; two of its local names are 'air-goat' and 'heather-bleater'; and I once stayed at a house whose owners had for years been puzzled by the mysterious herd of goats that in springtime they could hear but never see in the fields beyond a neighbouring wood. But surely this is an ignoble term for a sound of such mysterious intensity – a sound primeval and occult, with no domestic allusion? At all events, when the air rushed through the expanded tail feathers of the snipe above our Surrey garden, it was tom-toms, beaten in a remote valley and answered in the hollows of the intervening hills, that sounded in my childish ears.

Later, when the mist had gone, came the added delight of following the birds with our eyes. One after another they would rise from the meadows,

sometimes in twos and threes, and swing round and upward in ever-widening circles, their plumage gleaming now silver, now rufous red, as they faced or turned from the sun. Having breasted, as it seemed, a wave of the air, they would plunge earthward with downthrust beak and wings flung back, the throb and boom of the vibrant tail feathers becoming louder and louder as the pace of the dive increased, until each bird swung level just above the tree-tops and the sound broke off with the familiar shrill little buzz. Up they would go again with rapidly beating wings, so high that they almost reached vanishing point, to plunge and mount and plunge again. Sometimes their astonishing headers brought them to within three or four feet of the marsh, when they would hover for a few moments, the light catching the pale undersides of the wings, and call in excited tones – *chippi, chippi, chippi – chip, chip, chip,* – before they dropped into the rushes. I used to wonder – I do still – whether the spongey margins of the Bourne concealed a critical audience of their fellows, 'with store of ladies whose bright eyes' rained influence and judged the prize.

Many spring-time hours were beguiled in watching and listening to the snipe. When the days grew longer my father would stroll on to the lawn on fine evenings directly he got home from the City and look up at the birds as the lowering sunbeams caught and gilded their tireless wings. He was a little deaf and could not hear the 'drumming' except when a bird swooped low above his head; yet he seemed to sense it and the sight of the flying tournament brought him particular delight and relaxation. He once likened it to holidaymakers on a scenic railway and I have often thought his comparison apt for a performance that is so clearly a joy-ride. It was he who succeeded best in finding the cunningly hidden nests, with the beautiful blotched eggs, in shape like little pears, placed always with their narrow ends pointing inwards. He did not, as we did, wait in ambush behind one of the trees along the bottom of the garden, waiting for a bird to take off, trying to mark the spot by some rush or dead reed stem, then leaping the ditch and squelching towards the objective – only to find as we came nearer that this had mysteriously altered shape, or become one of several precisely similar clumps or stems. He depended on his sharp, experienced eyes and generally knew at a glance which little shadowy hollow would prove to be the footprint of a cow, a mere space between two tussocks, or the nest itself. More often than not a bird would spring up almost at our feet with that sharp exclamation which reminds me of linen being torn – with a quick wrench, not lingeringly in the manner of Smee! – and dash away in zig-zag flight, leaving us convinced after a fruitless search that, in my father's comforting words, 'It was only resting.' Later I developed with some success a technique of my own whenever I found myself in what we used to call 'snipey places'; this was to approach or walk across them with my eyes resolute on the ground about ten yards ahead, so that it was possible to fix with accuracy the point from which the bird rose. As one grows older, one becomes lazier and also, no doubt, wiser and refrains from the search; but if at the right season the birds do not happen to be joy-riding when I am in a likely habitat – which draining and reclamation have made increasingly rare in Southern England – I can seldom resist the temptation to try to put one up, for I have noticed that almost without fail it will proceed to give a display of aerobatics, to the accompaniment of those magical drum-rolls that none of my mother's children could hear without emotion.

A child's impressions are astonishingly persistent and can at times recreate the sounds and sights which produced them in a form so vivid as to haunt the mind with a sense of their continuing actuality. The meadows beyond our Surrey garden have long been drained and it must be many years since the snipe dived and drummed above the auburn-headed willows. Can it be that no one in that neighbourhood still enjoys that annual delight? Does not the faintest image or echo survive? Strange, when the very thought of a snipe drumming takes me back at once to the misty garden, where even now memory holds me waiting and alert; or to my bedroom on a moonlight night when my mother has just said good-night and through cupped hands blown out the candle. So bright is the radiance across my bed and so wakeful the world outside that sleep is not to be summoned. Presently I steal to the open casement and with my elbows on the white sill look out upon a garden transformed into silver and ebony and beyond to enchanted lagoons of floodwater that may have vanished by tomorrow. I listen entranced to wave upon wave of tremulous humming and hope for a glimpse of one whizzing arrow as it cuts across the disc of the moon.

HOME

o one would call the house where we were all born beautiful. It was built at a time – the mid eighteen-nineties – when however hard people tried to make beautiful things, or however confident they may have been of their success, the results have seldom excited the admiration of the following generations (though their critics have since put up many a building less pleasing to the eye). Brick predominated in its construction; it had tall chimneys, one with a cowl, and a red tiled roof; its upper storey was faced with pebble dash and beams set vertically at regular intervals; and the casement windows were filled with small rectangular panes. But as it faced east, south and west, its rooms caught and held all the daytime light; and when clothed with the jasmine and roses and honeysuckle that my mother had planted as a bride and surrounded by beds of the brightly coloured flowers that she loved, it had the indefinable air of friendliness and charm that goes with a happy disposition. It mattered not that its architecture was indifferent, even if we had noticed the fact. It was Home and we all loved it.

It had the great advantage of a beautiful position, on rising ground among fields; and from that gentle eminence, it looked out over a big garden that sloped down to the water-meadows whence the snipe took off on their thrilling aerobatics – meadows that stretched in ever-changing planes of green and gold and bronze to a middle distance of copses and single trees and tall, wayward hedges, and then away, far away, to the long line, sometimes dark blue, sometimes a shadowy grey, of the Surrey hills. Hyde Park Corner was hardly twenty miles away, but only when the trees were bare could another house be seen from the windows.

Its name was Pipers Hill, so whoever named it recognised that it stood a little above its surroundings; and if it had been called after some bygone owner of the land thereabout, surely the name would have had an apostrophe after the 'r'? As a child I never doubted that pipers had made music there in days of old, whether as accompanists to the clumsy hopping of 'rude mechanicals', or to the soundless tread of figures more etherial than themselves, elfin, shadowy and shy, content with music too thin for mortal ears to catch as it stole between the grass blades and over the fallen leaves – music that might still be heard in our own day, when the sun threw beams aslant into the garden hushed in stillness, the listener keeping as still as a flower on its stalk and his hands cupped to his ears. Once, at the far corner of the garden, where the narrow stream that we called the Ditch curved round the roots of an oak, I swear I did catch a tenuous skirl; but I must now suppose that, since I was noted in the family for imagining things, I had, like Sir Bedivere, heard only 'the ripple washing in the reeds'.

Leading from the drawing-room on the southern side of the house there was a verandah. From its ceiling in summer hung baskets of flowers, usually geraniums, but one contained a fuchsia, with flowers that wore purple and pink skirts in tiers and had long pendent stamens bright as gold. On warm summer evenings my mother would read to us there before bedtime and the stories of fun and adventure narrated in her quiet voice were lent a flavour and an undertone of garden scents and murmurs that made them sound different from those she read to us in the winter lamplight. The first of the evening's bats fluttered low, uttering its 'short, shrill, shriek', a great 'dumbledore' crashed onto one of the basket tables, a peewit called from the water-meadows and the scents of lavender and tobacco plant broke over us like waves. Or, in the afternoons, if it was not too hot to run about, or dig in the sandpit, or play my brother's favourite game of 'Order the Car', which entailed a great deal of pretence telephoning and a yet greater deal of physical exertion in his pedalled motor-car, I would pore over my book or drawing-block while the white butterflies flopped from grass to bush and the bees hummed and hummed among the rich blazoning of the sweet williams by the verandah steps. (How sharply in old age do these images pass across the screen of memory, as vivid as any that confront my present vision!)

Suddenly one day I was aware of a deeper hum and a more vibrant whirr of wings above my head and there, hovering beside the fuchsia was a moth I knew to be a humming-bird hawk. How was it that I knew? To tell how, I must be allowed a digression.

It was characteristic of my father's sense of fun that he would lend an air of mystery to certain names and phrases in constant use among the family by reducing them in speech or writing to their initial letters. This little game of his long preceded the craze for initialisation (if the word is allowable) that set in a few years before the last war. He would have thought this cheap and undignified; and how keen his sympathy would have been with a scholarly acquaintance of the family who in the later thirties was scandalised to see his own initials at the head of an article in *The Times* on *Air Raid*

*P*recautions!* But as children we shared my father's delight in the mystification, no less when all his mysteries had been revealed. We should, for example, have been sadly put out if birthday presents had not been accompanied by his best wishes for M.H.R.D.; if postcards from him had ended otherwise than with the letters L.F.D. (we never called him Father); or if, when the bright new silver coins, neatly folded in clean tissue paper, made their annual appearance in our places at the breakfast table on the morning of January 1st, the note inside had not borne the cryptic message H.N.Y.

My father most gleefully indulged this whim in the realm of entomology – the lepidopteral branch in particular. 'Run, boys, run!' he would exclaim, 'It's a C.Y.!' when his ever-alert eye caught a gleam of the yellow, chocolate-bordered wings of a clouded yellow butterfly glancing along the edge of an August oatfield among the plebeian M.B.s; and run we did. Again, on some open hill-top at evening, he would be the first to note the graceful flight of a painted lady as it circled round our group among the heather, remarking with delight when it settled: 'A.P.L. – and a perfect spec.' (pronounced to rhyme with dress). And naturally when we found ourselves in a likely stretch of woodland he would urge us to keep a sharp look out for a P.E.; but no matter how fervently each of us might H. for the B., no scion of that imperial family ever condescended to make our acquaintance.

It was, however, the initials of a moth that held the sharpest tingle of excitement as he pronounced them. 'Quick, boys, it's an H.B.H.M.' And there, hovering above the white bloom of a sea campion, on wings that vibrated so fast that they were no more than a silver-grey blur, would be a veritable humming-bird hawk-moth. That season when this ever fascinating migrant came to the fuchsia hanging from the roof of the verandah at home must have been a good year for its species. For by no means every year is favourable to it. Since then, in a lucky year I have watched them successively among sweet williams, red valerian, phlox or tobacco plants, sometimes lowering my head with caution to within a foot of the dynamic little aeronaut as it hangs whirring like an electric fan above a flower head, and as, with a superb combination of balance and marksmanship, it throws outward and downward its long curved tongue to probe the inmost recess and suck in the delicious fare. If it happens to come into the house it hurtles up and down the window panes at a rate and with a sound that demands the ever-popular word 'zoom' to describe it. Each time I have managed to catch the invader by placing a tumbler over it and slipping a thin card between the rim and the pane. Each time, all at once, the moth has lain still, giving me leisure to examine the beautiful grey-brown colour of the upper wings which, with

*The acquaintance was A.R. Powys, brother of John Cowper, T.F. and Llewelyn.

their delicately penned lines of black, resemble the bark of an oak; the flame-coloured crescents of the half-concealed hind-wings; and the long body proudly plumed with black and white. It has seemed to me, looking at my temporary captive, as if the glass enclosed a visible impulse of the energy that spins the world.

All such encounters take my mind back, not so much to the verandah fuchsia, as to childhood holidays in North Devon, when in the cuttings of the quaint broad-gauge railway that used to amble between Bideford and Appledore, an H.B.H.M. was quite often to be seen basking upon rocks almost too hot to touch, or hovering, as I have said, above the clumps of sea campion at the cliff verge, half way between blue sea and blue sky. At the end of an expedition, as we waited for the train at the halt above our favourite picnic place, an arrowy shape might dart along the platform, swerve towards a clump of sea pink where red-brown oak eggar caterpillars browsed or lay curled like a snail, and rush on to fling a lassoo of wings around the signal; or sometimes with an air of deliberate mockery one would charge the cow-catchered engine as it lumbered up. A minute or two later, when we had clambered up into the carriage and were seated on the slatted benches enveloped in our impedimenta of picnic baskets, haversacks, prawning and butterfly nets, camera, dog and what not, when the whistle had squealed and the engine had gasped into motion, the coach would rumble, and the wheels would begin to hum a rhythmic burden as they rolled along the track by the sea – a burden with a strangely familiar measure, to which every object in the carriage would rhythmically respond – H.B.H. *emm,* H.B.H. *emm,* H.B.H. – *emm.*

THE DEODAR

eyond the path in front of the verandah, which, as I have mentioned, led out of the drawing-room, there was a stretch of grass containing beds of wallflowers in the Spring and petunias and snapdragons in the Summer. This was known, rather grandly, as the 'upper' lawn, to distinguish it from the Lawn itself to which it descended by a low bank. The Lawn was just, but only just, big enough for a tennis court, but my parents were no good at any sort of game, nor were their children, whom they did what they could to encourage in such pursuits, so that tennis and croquet were indulged in (I can think of no more appropriate word) at infrequent intervals and in moods of hilarity hardly ever punctuated by sulks or bursts of irritation. Nor were our sessions at pat-ball, as my father without meaning to be unkind called our attempts at tennis, improved by our white mongrel dog, who, even in old age, would be spurred to ecstasies of delight by our antics, rushing this way and that to seize a ball and carry it off into the Wild Patch, a thicket of shrubs and long grass which lay beyond another and much steeper bank. Both banks, however, sported charming little wild flowers in their sandy soil: blue devil's-bit scabious, yellow hawkbit and rufous sheep's sorrel, all haunted by small copper butterflies and azure 'blues' and by delightful silver Y moths which, unlike the majority of their *confrères*, enjoy flying by day – their brown and grey wings a-whirr from early morning to sundown, at rest only now and again to enjoy some specially sweet drop of nectar; and it is then that you can see the glittering letter on the upper wing that gives the moth its name. The banks also boasted – perhaps a little to their (and our) shame – patches of flourishing moss, which threw up slender stems topped with silvery hoods. These, when pulled off, revealed delicately modelled statuettes like chess-men, green as jade: I regret never having learnt what species of moss it was. When we did not occupy the Lawn with either our attempts at formal games, or others of our own invention, it was a veritable rink or dance-floor for pied wagtails – but I will come to them later.

To one side of the upper lawn there was a big bush of pampas grass which my mother disliked, but as my father persisted in admiring the triumphant plumes it vaunted every Autumn it was allowed to stay. On the opposite side there was a large circular clump of rhododendrons backed by a tall deodar. This fine tree played various parts in our games, its layered shades being admirably designed for hide-and-seek, or for sequestered sessions of reading to oneself. One year, to our great delight, a pair of golden-crested wrens chose a branch on which to hang their mossy hammock of a nest stuffed full of feathers. I would watch the dimunitive khaki-clad figures, in bright fore-and-aft caps, darting this way and that with the wayward grace of a feather borne on the impulse of the lightest current of air. As often as not they would hang upside down, then suddenly spring into the air and hover with wing beats as rapid as a hawk-moth's. The song, a tenuous thread of high-pitched demi-semi-quavers, seemed to go winding along like the whirr of the old Singer sewing-machine in the nursery, and as I listened I became aware of the dark, looming immensity of the place the tiny creatures had chosen as that season's home. The thought startled me: one of the tree's cones, small enough to me, would in their sight be as large as a great boulder.

A pair used to nest every year in the garden of my preparatory school. The Headmaster, who was a keen naturalist, knew the bird by sight, but could not hear its song: its pitch was too high for his not-so-young ears. I see myself standing beside him beneath the tree where the nest was, and dis-respectfully nudging him whenever the bird sang. At every nudge he would hollow his hand to his ear, but in vain, until I was fairly dancing with impatience and incredulity. He used to say that I grew far more impatient with him over his obtuseness in not hearing the goldcrest's song than he ever did with me over my failure to conjugate a Latin or Greek verb. Now the whirligig of time has brought in his revenges! My own ears have grown old or obtuse, so that I watch the beak opening, but can hear no sound.

Some years later, the same Headmaster, by then retired, inveigled me, by then an undergraduate, into helping him take a party of schoolgirls on a nature ramble in Dorset, where he lived. Before we set out we decided on a division of labour; he was to point out the flowers and butterflies and I the birds. In a neighbouring wood he soon found a number of interesting plants – including that dusky beauty, a bird's-nest orchid – but as the party crashed through the undergrowth I began to despair of bringing the girls within sight or sound of a bird. Suddenly my ear detected the unmistakable whisper of a goldcrest, and I managed to call for silence and a halt. The little bird is, in fact, remarkably tame and within a few seconds it had whisked down onto a low branch of the larch near which we were all standing.

'Listen carefully now,' I commanded, 'and you will hear the song of our smallest native bird, a golden-crested wren.' I held up my hand. The youthful ears all about had no difficulty in hearing the song and there were expressions of delight most gratifying to the young impresario.

'With luck,' I went on, somewhat in the confident manner of a conjuror about to perform a trick, 'we might find its nest.' I looked up and there, about two feet above my head, was indeed the familiar little mossy hammock. I paused a moment to gain the full effect.

'Yes,' I proclaimed, 'and here it is.'

Did ever a conjuror listen to greater gasps of astonishment? If life has held few successes for me, I can at least count upon one; and since then my affection for the goldcrest has retained a special warmth.

But there was something in the air that afternoon; how rarely is Life, or Chance, disposed to repeat a stroke of luck! Our 'ramble' proceeded to a stretch of rough open ground, a sort of common, known locally as The Prairie, where there were little quarries and hummocks and smooth stretches of flower-embroidered grass between thickets of bracken. It was bugle-time, and there were plentiful groups of that beautiful little pagoda-like flower spread about in patches bluer than blue. (It is a colour that has no exact likeness: Hopkins somewhere uses the term 'bugle-blue'.) In the middle of one such patch there had settled a small butterfly – one of a species that is not exactly rare, but is uncommon enough to give a butterfly-lover a tingle of excitement whenever he sees one. Whoever named it appreciated its aristocracy, giving it the title of The Duke of Burgundy fritillary.* Like other fritillaries, this miniature has wings of tawny gold latticed with darkest brown or black, so it will be imagined how brilliantly the speck I was looking at showed against its backcloth of blue.

I had seen it before my old friend and pointing it out to him I whispered, 'It's your turn.' At once he replied with a smile, 'I think the girls would prefer *you* to show it to them.'

So I did, having first martialled them in a circle round the tiny, seemingly unconscious creature. Unconscious! The gasps of surprise and delight had an immediate effect, for it began to close and open and close its wings, repeating the movement again and again as if fully aware of its beauty and preening itself on this sudden wave of adulation. When we had all gazed our fill, or it had decided that we had, it just flew away.

---

*See illustration on page 1.

THE LAWN

ied wagtails, as I have mentioned, took great delight in our lawn and as athletes were far superior to us. My mother had a special affection for this graceful and agile bird which she called a 'dish-washer'; I don't quite see the reason for this term, though in some odd way it is apt. Yet I prefer the nick-name a Somerset farmer's wife gave it – 'Trotty' or 'Little trotty wagtail'. With what effortless speed it can and does trot! If my memory is not at fault, when Fred Astaire and his sister Adèle first came to London in the early twenties, they delighted and dazzled their audience with an extremely quick dance called a 'something-Trot' – I just cannot call to mind the adjective, and certainly I think of them both, Fred in particular, when I watch a pied wagtail dancing across the grass. Our Trotty also, as other trotties do, used to whisk along the roof-ridge, tail a-bobbing, and springing now and then into the air would spin round the black cowl that topped our centre chimney. In Spring a sudden chirrup from somewhere high up among the tiles would announce the bird's arrival before we had seen it scamper across the grass above its gliding shadow. Certainly it is on level grass that the bird, with its slender, black-stockinged legs, shows its twinkling paces to the best advantage. Those black stockings remind me of some Toulouse-Lautrec figure dancing the can-can – except that she has an air of decadent sophistication quite alien to innocent Trotty. We only once found her nest – somehow I usually think of the bird as 'she' – and that was in a curious place in an insalubrious environment. Even though the house was so near London it was not on main drainage, and in one part of the garden there was a cesspit enclosed by a somewhat crazy structure cloaked in ivy. For obvious reasons we did not look very closely in its dark umbrage for birds' nests, but one day Trotty flew out as we passed and I determined to explore. A little above my head was a blackbird's dis-used nest, cracked and tousled, but something prompted me to make a closer examination, and straining up I peered over the rim. There, within the broken cup was another, neat and rounded, made of thin grass stems and

23

lined with horsehair, containing four or five white eggs speckled over with black. So this was Trotty's choice for her current home.

I have had various encounters with trotties since: one, long after my childhood had ended and at a critical moment in our country's fortunes, lingers in mind. In late August 1939, I was staying in Yorkshire with an old friend. We spent the morning after I arrived fitting the tenants, old and young, on the small estate with gas-masks; later, as a relief, the warm, still afternoon inclined me to nothing more strenuous than some desultory reading, and the quiet enjoyment of the timeless atmosphere of the old house and garden. Little or no activity broke the stillness save that of the resident trotties on the broad stretch of grass in front of the house. Presently my hostess pushed her mother, aged over ninety, in her wheeled chair out onto the lawn and to a sheltered place dappled with the shadows of 'Napoleon's larch', the seed of which the Emperor had given to one of her forebears. Shortly afterwards, my hostess's father, almost a centenarian – a 'colossal wreck' of a man who made me think of the fallen statue of Ozymandias – was pushed out in his chair by his man-servant, and set beside his wife. The old couple sat beside each other in silence, since she could not raise her soft voice above a whisper, and this he was too deaf to hear. But they remained side by side an hour or more, his right hand clasped in her left. A few yards away the wagtails jaunted, the two silent watchers following with evident delight their runs and sallies and sudden leaps into the air.

When we had finished tea, which had been brought out to the summer-house, and as the sun had gone in, the old couple were wheeled back into the house. A little later I joined the old lady in the drawing-room, where she was seated in a high-backed chair, a silk scarf round her shoulders and a tortoiseshell kitten on her lap. While her delicate fingers, as white as the ivory keys on the piano beside her, played over the soft warm-coloured fur, she began to tell me of the adventures she and her mother had had in Frankfurt at the time of the Austro-Prussian War of 1866. She recalled how at the opera people wore badges coloured black, red and white, symbolising 'out of darkness through bloodshed into light'; how she had concealed hers at the bottom of her trunk when they were conveyed in a Prussian troop train to Coblenz; and how when at last they reached Rotterdam and decided that, as there were a few days of their holiday still to run, they would not take the weekly packet-boat to England, they learnt that the city was in the grip of an epidemic of cholera.

Her reminiscences were cut short by the obligation to listen to the latest news bulletin from the B.B.C. Our ambassador in Berlin, Sir Neville Henderson, had returned to London with a report of his latest meeting with the Führer: Japan for some reason was angry; Spain cold; Hungary flinching;

Hitler had received telegrams from the Pope and President Roosevelt; King Victor Emanuele had offered mediation; Canada, Australia and New Zealand had each pledged support for the Mother Country in the event of War. Was any gleam of hope to be decried in these exchanges?

When the bulletin was over, I went out into the fresh air, and on the lawn the wagtails were as active as ever. Presently my hostess joined me and asked if I would spare a few minutes to go and talk to her father. I found him sprawled in a tall chair, his great figure slouched forward and his leonine head bent over his chest. He greeted me with a loud bark, and waving his hand to a chair beside the table in front of him, bade me write on a note-pad anything I wished to say. How vapid one's observations look when set down on paper with a blunt pencil! Fortunately, he wished to do the talking and being in a narrative mood he soon launched into an account of how he had been sent as a boy to stay with an uncle stationed in Gibraltar. He had been there barely a week before his uncle received instructions to join his regiment in the Crimea, where the war had just started. There was nothing for it but to take the boy with him. The old man's voice rose as he recalled the excitement of the voyage out and his eyes lit up as he described the glow of the Russian camp-fires in front of Sebastopol. So vivid did he make it all that I fancied I could see flames gleaming at points across the big estate-map on the wall behind him. . . . Then the gong sounded for dinner and I left him sprawled in his chair, his white mane illumined by the oil-lamp the man-servant had brought silently in.

As I waited alone in the drawing-room among the crowded relics of past years, some from the Crimea it might be, others from the dominions of the Emperor Francis Joseph, others from earlier times – that piano, for instance, which Mendelssohn had presented to great-grandmamma as a girl, or Great Aunt Henrietta's water-colours, joint products of herself and her teacher, David Cox – I began to wonder in what era I now found myself, and to cherish a transient hope that it was not the actual one, dark with apprehension of what the next few days might bring. Even though dusk was falling I could see through the window the wagtails, untroubled by any such apprehension, still busily trotting to and fro across this other lawn.

THE DRIVE

he approach to the house was by way of a straight lane about two hundred yards long which we grandly called the Avenue. At a pair of white gates, balustraded along their upper halves and solid below, it became the Drive, a nearly semi-circular stretch of gravel leading to the front door. The chord of the segment was a dark, narrow path leading back to the white gates, known always in the singular as the White Gate, and the segment itself was occupied by the Shrubbery, a plantation of laurels, silver dogwoods, lilacs, a maple and a laburnum. Tradesmen, as a rule, were not permitted to come up the Drive; they left their carts or vans at the White Gate and carried their goods up the path to the Yard on the north side of the house, where they were received by Cook at the kitchen door. Only some exalted vehicle, like Harrods' delivery van, rolled up the Drive to the front door.

The Shrubbery was a great place for nests. Every year a blackbird or a song-thrush built there and almost always a chaffinch. The laurels had grown lanky and were climbable, so that one could scramble up to a point of vantage in a crotch of the blackish-green boughs and see the eggs lying snug; and if one were cautious and patient enough to stay very still, one could watch the hen return to brood, rounding her body to the cup of the nest and making a shovelling motion as she settled the eggs comfortably beneath her breast. At the same level as one's own, a bird's eye is wonderfully round and black.

The dark side-path was sunless and a little frightening. Was it the spot where lurked, according to Mrs Alexander's hymn, the 'wicked spirit' that was 'watching round you still'? True it was lit in spring by the pink and white blossom of a cherry-apple-tree and the fiery scarlet of its fruit in autumn, and as the path had ruts it made an exciting glissade for our toy car propelled by furious pedalling. But the path has retained for me one disagreeable association. I had been an implicit believer in fairies and all their radiant activities,

27

but it was in that path that my brother, with no consciousness of ill intent, assured me that there were no such things as fairies; the fairies who decorated the nursery after we had gone to bed on Christmas Eve were Mother and Nurse and Lily the housemaid – he had seen them at work. Aghast, I felt the tears begin to well up and overflow and in my misery I cried, 'They'll be telling me next that Jesus and Mary and Moses and all the people in the Bible aren't true either.' Others, more sophisticated than my brother, have tried to do that since; but then, confounded by my outburst, he sought to comfort me by allowing me a longer spell than usual in the car, and it was not long before I had pedalled away my distress.

A thuya hedge ran round the curve of the Drive opposite to the Shrubbery and as often as not, when I see or listen to a greenfinch or a hedge-sparrow, which both nested in it every year, my mind's eye glimpses its bottle-green folds and – if the mind has a nose – I catch a waft of its sharp, piney smell.

It is hardly possible in speaking of the greenfinch not to mention Wordsworth, for though the poet, *qua* naturalist, nodded now and again, I do not know any poem which more exactly captures the essence of a bird than the one called 'The Green Linnet', and I have little doubt but that his sister Dorothy – the 'exquisite sister' – had been sitting with him on 'the orchard seat' in the 'sequestered nook' and had then, as so often, given him the eyes to see the bird as she saw it – and ears, too, to listen as they watched:

> *A Life, a Presence like the Air,*
> *Scattering thy gladness without care,*
> *Too blest with anyone to pair;*
> *   Thyself thy own enjoyment . . .*
>
> *Behold him perched in ecstasies*
> *   Yet seeming still to hover;*
> *There! where the flutter of his wings*
> *Upon his back and body flings*
> *Shadows and sunny glimmerings,*
> *   That cover him all over.*

The lilt of the verse exactly responds to the lilt of the song and of the bird's movements. The greenfinch is an early singer and a late nester, and there would still be a nestful of bright-eyed young among the thuya's green folds in the summer holidays when the tobacco plants my mother used to plant beneath it were blowing from their white trumpets blasts of scent that seemed almost to throb in the evening air. One late August morning many

years later, in a Somerset and not a Surrey garden, when, precariously balanced on a pair of steps, I was clipping a ball on top of a yew hedge – or as
near a ball as an unskilled topiarist could make it – I saw inside the ball a
wodge of moss and grass rimmed with a frieze of bright eyes. There was
nothing for it but to give up my work for the time being until the fledgling
greenfinches had achieved enough feathers to fly away. The greenfinch's first
song is, it must be confessed, a blend of a sneeze and a sneer – almost as if
like a very different personage, Pooh Bah, he was 'born sneering' – but the
sound being one of Spring's heralds, I cannot but greet it with a cheer now,
as in the days when it came again and again from the thuya hedge along the
Drive, or from the blossoming apple-tree just beyond.

The hedge-sparrow is a very different bird. I am aware that I ought not to
use that name, because although he – and I deliberately use the personal
pronoun – spends so much of his time in hedges, such as our thuya, he is not
a sparrow; but as children we could not get used to the term 'dunnock', by
which the bird is properly known – still less could we stomach the pedantic
'hedge accentor' – and so we invented the diminutive 'hedgie', which could
be prefixed by 'Mr' or 'Mrs' as the sex of the bird required. (It is in fact almost
impossible to distinguish the sexes by sight, but we presumed it was 'Mr'
who sang and 'Mrs' who brooded the eggs.) The nickname seemed an exact
expression of our affectionate feelings towards a bird of such a modest,
gentle and retiring disposition – though I must admit I have noticed a more
assertive side when a rival ventures to infringe territorial rights.* Although he
appears to be sober-suited, when you examine his plumage closely you find
a rich combination of purplish grey, black and deep chestnut brown, and his
little straight legs, kept strictly parallel as he hops along, are as red as
embers. But whatever 'hedgies' may lack of brilliant colours in their person
the debit is far over-balanced by the splendour of the eggs: blue, green-blue,
blue-green, as you will, like sea-water in a cavern of black rocks. The nest is
one of the cosiest and most comfortable-looking of all, the cup thickly lined
with moss and perfectly rounded; and as Spring is the time for hanging out
carpets on clothes-lines to be whacked in the sunshine, we would find that
tufts of blue or red wool had been added as embroidery. Mr Hedgie is also a
compulsive singer, for he will sing in all weathers and, almost, at all times
and seasons. The song is high-pitched and runs in hurried phrases: we tried
in vain to find words for them; and it was not until many years later that a
friend, who was himself a sensitive writer of both poetry and prose, told me
that he had often tried to do the same, but had been obliged to fall back on

---

*Appearances can be deceptive and no one, it seems, is above suspicion. I have read lately that
a Mrs Hedgie is sometimes known to take a lover! Until I myself have caught one *in flagrante* I
shall continue to disbelieve the slur.

the rigmarole printed in the *Handbook*: '*weeso, sissi-weeso, sissi-weeso, sissi-weeso.*' Well, I suppose the rhythm is about right!

Hedgie figured in an unforgotten incident one Spring holiday at Studland. On the top of a scrupulously neat privet hedge in front of a scrupulously neat cottage, my brother and I saw the familiar little bird singing proudly away and felt sure that he must have a nest close by, so we peered this way and that into the leafy recesses in the hope of finding it. Suddenly there was a sharp click and in the gateway stood a tall, thin, Betsy Trotwood-like figure, the sun striking steel-rimmed disapproval from her spectacles, and on the top of the large, flat bun on the crown of her head was a large, flat hat skewered with a ferocious hat-pin: we agreed afterwards that the nob sparkled like the hilt of Excalibur.

'Now, you boys, *what,* may I ask, are you doing?'

'Er – nothing,' my brother replied.

'It stands to reason you *must* have been doing SOMETHING.'

Silence. 'Well?' she continued in tones that boded nothing but ill. 'I am waiting for an answer.'

Another silence. Then my brother gave me a sharp nudge, and in a perfectly concerted action we both raised our caps and fled. We were careful not to look for nests in that part of the village again; and the pronouncement beginning 'It stands to reason' became a catch-phrase which, when any explanation is required, remains in force to this day.

I must end my little eulogy of 'hedgie' by another in a letter long ago from my old friend the Headmaster of my preparatory school. I had written previously to tell him that my wife was expecting our first child and he was now replying to a second letter telling him how she – how we both! – was getting on. 'Poor human beings!' he wrote: 'What a laborious proceeding the production of life is compared with that of many other living creatures! This has been particularly brought home to me by this little incident: I watched a pair of hedge-sparrows engaged in building their nest just below the drawing-room window, about two feet away. On Easter Day it was finished and I showed it to a small boy, aged 10, who had called upon me all on his own because he had heard I had not been well. On seeing it from the window he said, 'Gosh, how ripping!' On Wednesday, 28th April, the first blue egg was laid and on Sunday, May 2nd, the last; then the little mother sat very close for 12 days, and the great event took place. In the next ten days nothing was to be seen but wide open mouths. On the 11th day, May 25th, when I was examining the nest, I saw instead of a mouth a most intelligent little pair of eyes looking at me with beak closed, and another pair beside it. Later that morning my housekeeper came to me where I was planting lettuces and said, "The little birds are out and all over the garden;" and so they were – a month

31

before there was nothing and now four most spritely little birds. I am not at all sure that the dunnock is not my favourite of all birds. It has all the qualities that a good Christian ought to have: Happiness (listen to its little song); modesty (look at its unadorned but very beautiful plumage); patience (watch the parent birds); industry (never are they unemployed); and especially observe that they always *mind their own business*, which Christians often do not do. But why was it not ordained for the human race to reproduce itself in the same way?'

THE AVENUE

t was in a blackthorn bush on one side of the Avenue that I first looked into a wild bird's nest. Our nurse at that time found it. She had come to us as a country girl from Norfolk when I was hardly out of the cradle, and over the years she took turns to be nursery-maid, nurse, housemaid and cook – my father called her 'the quick-change artist'. She was tall and thin and rather gruffly-spoken, with very long arms which made her a champion picker of blackberries, and they were adept also at grabbing an elusive child or giving a dreamy 'slow-coach' a salutary shove: they could well have administered a salutary slap, but I do not recall that they ever did.

On our walk that April morning we must have set out with the express object of 'birds-nestin'', for she suddenly exclaimed, 'And here's a booty!' as she parted the prickly branches. She lifted us in turns to look into the nest, and I have never forgotten the sight of the blue, black-spotted eggs lying in their brown cup, so smoothly rounded and modelled, and enclosed in an outer basin of interwoven grasses and moss, and all around and above it the clusters of starry white blossoms.

Maybe because of that very early association, which kindled a lifelong interest in birds' nests and eggs and an unfaltering joy in finding them, I have always thought a song-thrush's nest – for such it was – to be one of the most admirable of all. It has not the finely wrought construction nor the exquisite decoration of, for example, the nests of a chaffinch, a goldfinch or a long-tailed tit, nor, I suppose, would it be so comfortable to grow up in, though it would be more airy; but as a simple object, perfectly framed for its purpose and without frills or refinements, it has for me the direct appeal of a good pot. The clear-eyed John Clare delighted in it:

> *How true she warped the moss to form a nest*
> *And modelled it within with wood and clay;*

And by and by, like heath-bells gilt with dew
There lay her shining eggs, as bright as flowers
Ink-spotted over shells of greeny blue.

The little poem from which these lines are taken was included by George Moore, Walter de la Mare and John Freeman in their *Anthology of Pure Poetry*. Perhaps that is what I am trying to say: the nest with a quartet of eggs in it is a piece of pure poetry.

Not that I think much less of the nests of the two other most common members of the thrush family, the mistle-thrush and the blackbird. A mistle-thrush built every year in a tree in our churchyard, in what I might call a 'classic' position for its species, since the nest was placed in the first and wide open crook of the slender trunk, hardly six feet from the ground, and with no cover or additional twig: we could never understand how the first grass stems the bird collected stayed in position or, for that matter, the completed nest to which she always added a piece of white rag or paper as a sort of trade-mark. Since then I have found nests in much loftier positions and also even lower down: once in the wall of a ruined chapel in Ireland, a place so melancholy and withdrawn, so full of long departed yet half perceived presences, that a mistle-thrush's nest lent a touch of the familiar and the everyday. And once, in a gorse bush near the sea in North Devon, where the pale blue eggs, so softly mottled in browns and greys and purples, made with the golden splendour of the furze-blooms and the deeper blue of the springtime sea beyond a colour harmony that has lived in memory. As for blackbirds' nests, which we found almost everywhere – in banks and hedges, in ivy-tods and straw-stacks, in the potting-shed and 'coach-house', among grass tussocks and tree-roots and piles of pea-sticks – they were always, with their clutches of freckled eggs, just dear and taken for granted, even to the point of inducing a slight sense of disappointment when a nest entailing a scratchy climb or scramble to reach it evoked the cry of 'It's only an old blackie.' Blackie was the gardener's name for the bird. 'Have you,' he once asked, 'seen the blackie's nest in the "rosy-dandrums"?'

The blackbird, however, bears away the bell as a singer: I place him even above the nightingale, whose voice has astonished listeners through the ages by the richness and agility of its coloratura and moved them by the supposed outpourings of 'eternal passion, eternal pain' that gush from the 'tawny-throated'. Indeed, as delightful as any poem is the prose eulogy of Auceps in *The Compleat Angler*: 'But the Nightingale, another of my airy creatures, breathes such sweet loud musick out of her little instrumental throat, that it might make mankind to think miracles are not ceased. He that at midnight, when the very labourer sleeps securely, should hear, as I have very often, the clear airs, the sweet descants, the natural rising and falling, the doubling and redoubling of her voice, might well be lifted above earth, and say, Lord, what musick hast thou provided for the Saints in Heaven, when thou affords to bad men such musick on Earth!'

But it was the opening staves of a blackbird's song, the bird itself invisible at the far end of a garden long ago, as they stroked the hushed twilight of a February evening, that first awakened a child's consciousness to the searching beauty of the sound and moved him to sudden disconcerting tears. It is a song that above all others expresses the transient nature of all things, the linked phrases telling out note by note and with every passing moment how time steals along. A child's first impressions have a poignant insistence; and now, in old age, no sound moves me more deeply than the bird's first utterance of the year, the quiet music floating across another garden far distant in time and place from the lawn where it first haunted my imagination.

It cannot be denied that, as a personality – the cock at any rate – the bird is a bit of a 'fuss-pot'; that is what, as children, we called him, feeling both amused and vexed at the way he flounced his wings and wagged his tail as he scolded the other birds at bed-time with his irritable *'tchack – tchacking'*: I used to wait for my aunts, when they came to stay, to exclaim, 'Just hark at the night-watchman!' But having, as I fancied, bundled the other birds into bed, he would resume the golden melody for a while until darkness closed his beak and his eyes in sleep. Now, when the dog days come and the song falters and dies away, I grow sad, knowing that five or six months must pass before, if I am fortunate enough, a chilly dusk will restore to my ears and heart those first wistful notes once again. Tennyson, it will be remembered, professed to love the song and kept his blackhearts unnetted so that the bird's 'gold dagger of a bill' was left free 'to fret the summer's jenneting'; but there is a touch of smugness in his claim and something more genuine in Addison's bluff declaration: 'I value my garden more for being full of blackbirds than of cherries, and very frankly give them fruit for their songs.'

When friends, not specially interested in birds, have asked me to distinguish for them the songs of the song-thrush, the blackbird and the mistlethrush, I have attempted an analogy from music. The song-thrush, so it seems to me, is the Mozart, the blackbird the Schubert or the Schumann, and the mistle-thrush the Wagner. The song-thrush, unlike the other two, sings phrases that one can put into words: for example: 'Pretty dear, pretty dear, pretty *little* dear!' (Is this not the very phrasing of the opening theme of Mozart's Symphony No. 40?) The blackbird's has the flowing measure that Schubert and Schumann have at effortless command: that of, let us say, the piano postlude to Schumann's song-cycle *Dichterliebe*; whereas the mistlethrush, the dauntless 'storm-cock', pouring out from a tree-top on a windy

March day a stream of notes that can ride out a gale, makes me think of Brünnhilde's voice breasting the surge and spume of *The Ring*'s orchestral waves.

GOLDFINCHES, CAPTIVE AND FREE

nother bird's nest that I associate with the Avenue is the goldfinch's. A few yards further along from the blackthorn hedge, but on the opposite side, there was a pink may-tree, and one year a pair of goldfinches nested in it. Steps were brought along to reach it and one had to stand precariously on the unsteady platform at the top to look in and see the eggs: these were of the palest sea-green, encircled at the larger end with a ring of tiny markings the colour, as I used to think, of strawberry jam. The nest itself was – and indeed always is – a marvel of intricate construction, being tightly woven of grass and moss and horsehair, with a feather or two tucked in for good measure: I remember once finding one on the ground which had been blown out of a tree, and its texture was as tough as a piece of felt. The nest in the may-tree also made an unforgettable impression on me, surrounded this time not with white, but with chubby rosy-cheeked blossoms which seemed to change colour every moment as the sunlight glinted among the fingered leaves.

I have a partiality for goldfinches. They are among the most talented of birds: they excel in flight, in song and in architecture and combine with neatness of person and beauty of plumage qualities defined long ago by Buffon as 'sagacity and docility of disposition' – qualities, alas, which have so often condemned them to captivity. The number of their nicknames bears witness to their popularity: 'Knicker', 'Sheriff's man', 'gowdspink' and 'redcap' are a few.

'In a state of confinement,' Bewick says of goldfinches in the text to one of his liveliest engravings, 'they are very engaging, being much attached to their keepers, and will learn a variety of little tricks, such as to draw up buckets containing their water and food, to fire a cracker and suchlike.' Such tricks are little to our taste today, but they may well have influenced Hardy's sometime mayor of Casterbridge in the choice of a caged goldfinch as a wedding present for the girl whom he had so long deceived with the belief that she was his daughter; the gift miscarried and the Wessex novels contain no keener shaft of sadness than the discovery of the prisoner, dwindled by starvation to 'a little ball of feathers', forgotten in the press of larger human sorrows.

Many years after that first acquaintance with a goldfinch's nest, at a time when things were going wrong with my work in London, I used to go for short periods to the National Gallery and the chance discovery of a goldfinch in Crivelli's resplendent altar-piece, now named after Prince Anatole Demidorff, who put its components together in the first half of the last century, set me off on a search for goldfinches in other pictures in the Gallery. The bird in Crivelli's painting fascinated me, since for once the bird had a gloomy and disconsolate air, expressing an unaccustomed listlessness and disgust for life, which happened to reflect my own mood at the time. And then, in another painting by Crivelli on the far side of the room – *The Vision of the Blessed Gabrieli* – I found the same little goldfinch, in the same dejected attitude, turning its back upon the world. This set me wondering why Crivelli twice introduced into his paintings a bird of this species and in a form so uncharacteristic, and what symbolism, if any, one might read into it. Perhaps the bird was a pet, full of the sagacity that Buffon spoke of, and subject to moods of unwarranted disgust when, in return for all his pretty tricks and carillons of song, his master went on and on painting. Or could it have been that Crivelli used it as an emblem of some occasional black mood of his own in which, for a moment despairing of his powers, he felt impelled to turn his back on art and the world?

It may be that we see the very cage the bird occupied, hanging from the bar above the first-floor balcony of the Madonna's house in the artist's portrayal of *The Annunciation*. A bird of some sort can be seen between the bars, and though it is set so high that identification is difficult, there is a telltale touch of red and a gleam of yellow which point to its being a goldfinch. One may hope that this bird, though a proclaimed captive unlike the others, is not indifferent to the momentous happening below, but celebrates the discharge and acceptance of the Divine mission with a shower of those brilliant notes which sound when they come to us in the open by orchard or hedgerow, like the twangling instruments that baffled and entranced Caliban, or as if the bars of gold on the wings were in truth the clinking metal.

I can recommend a search for goldfinches in the pictures at the National Gallery – or elsewhere for that matter – since it can bring delightful rewards: Carpaccio, Benozzo Gozzoli and Baroccio all noted the bird with pleasure. Their renderings convey all the multi-coloured gaiety of plumage that calls to mind the charming Polish legend of the goldfinch waiting in line with the other newly-created birds to be painted by God; of how it grew restless and played truant, but returned at length, only to find the work done and the company dispersed; how in tears it begged to be decorated like the rest and how the Almighty relented and gave the plumage a dab of all the colours left on His palette. In particular, I advise the many people who never tire of looking over the low hill and meadow, forest and glittering water, where the *Chateau de Steen* raises its towers and gabled roofs, to look again at the bottom right hand corner of the picture. The eyes of the lordly, cosmopolitan Rubens took in the miniature with the grand in nature, and he has given the last touch of truth to his late summer scene by introducing at that point in the composition a charm of goldfinches among the bushes. His handling is impressionist, but the dabs of bright colour coalesce to form the fluttering shapes of the birds – one hovering, one balanced on a twig, one darting towards a clump of ragwort. It is a pleasant surmise that Rubens, as he sat at his easel in the bland sunshine, sketching out the draft of his great painting, put down his brush for a moment to enjoy the delicate antics and sweet sparkling music of the little flock that drifted fortuitously by, and decided there and then to repay them for the pleasure they brought him by granting them the immortality of his paint. As Keats was to do, in another medium, for the birds that delighted him one happy day in another century:

> *Sometimes goldfinches one by one will drop*
> *From low hung branches; little space they stop;*
> *But sip, and twitter, and their feathers sleek;*
> *Then off at once, as in a wanton freak;*
> *Or perhaps, to show their black and golden wings,*
> *Pausing upon their yellow flutterings.*

Picture lovers more travelled than I am will know of painted goldfinches in other galleries. I recall one of the most illustrious of the kind – the bird that gives its name to Raphael's *Madonna del Cardellino* in the Uffizi – and one (seen long ago) clutched almost to suffocation in the hand of the infant Jesus in Montagna's *Madonna and Child* in the Ashmolean; and I cannot forbear to say a word about the noblest goldfinch of them all, whose portrait by Carel Fabritius, Rembrandt's gifted pupil, hangs in the Mauritshuis and came last to England for the Winter Exhibition at Burlington House in 1952/3. The picture has a sad incidental connection in that it is clearly dated 1654, the year of the artist's untimely death in an explosion. The dignity and pathos of the captive, patient and innocently reproachful, are conveyed with wonderful skill; its form so gaily coloured, so light and feathery and warm with life, ready at a moment to leap singing into the air, yet tethered by the inexorable chain. It is the image of Michael Henchard's hapless bird.

GLADDY

he hedges on either side of the Avenue and around the fields that lay next to it were graced by another favourite bird of mine, the yellow-hammer. It was not common there, as it is in downland, or among the lanes of Devonshire where I associate it with family holidays, but its scarcity made us the fonder of the few birds that made their home near ours. The song, first heard in February, when its cheerful notes glittered like stars in the low-hung gloom, seemed full of promise that spring would not fail to come. On and on it went in its tripping measure through the summer and well into September, when the corn had been cut and blackberries were glossy beneath the singer on his hedge-top perch, head thrown back and wings a-quiver, giving so clear an assurance of his own gladness that the listener could not but feel glad too.

It was indeed the driver of the wagonette on excursions to Clovelly and Hartland whose name for our Avenue birds was 'Gladdy'. As we trundled along and one singing yellow-hammer passed on its song like a torch to another, he would point with his whip and remark in his broad Devon: 'Butiful little birds, they gladdies, bless their hearts! They'm always cheerful, I reckon. Glad they be and glad they do make us.' The successive trills were as continuous as the fragrance of the honeysuckle drifting from the tall road-side hedges. They came to us, now loud, now soft, now loud again, as we rumbled along, sitting sideways, knee to knee beneath the stable-smelling rug; or when at the foot of a steep hill the horses' load needed lightening, we had scrambled out onto the dusty road and were tramping beside the wheels. I used to fancy that those gold-crowned birds had forgotten just then their habitual plea for a morsel of cheeseless bread and were anxious only for us to get on and make the most of our outing. 'Best-of-luck-but-step-along . . . *please!*' they seemed to chant.

If our destination were Hartland, there was usually a long walk back from the cliffs in the evening by lanes whose hedges were entwined with honey-

41

suckle and bursting with blackberries, nuts and sloes – lanes that turned and twisted like hunted hares. It was then that the repetitive song took on a hint of mockery and the words of the nursery rhyme began to haunt my mind:

> *How many miles to Babylon?*
> *Three score miles and ten.*
> *Can I get there by candle-light?*
> *Yes, and back again.*

I wondered whether the birds went on singing after sunset and whether each of the yellow heads sent out a flickering beam in the darkness to light the way.

Suddenly, when we least expected, the lane would give a hop, skip and a jump and pitch us straight into the village. Within a few minutes we were all inside the inn and ranged round the big table, spread to the floor with a white cloth, and waiting for a moment of jubilation. This was the arrival of the Cackling Hen. She did not in truth so far demean herself as to cackle, for she was made of china: a plump, bunting shape, imperious of eye, her plumage a deep glossy brown and lavishly sprigged with gold; and the barge-like nest she sat in if not of 'beaten gold' was near enough a 'burnished throne'. Maud, the parlourmaid, would bear her in and place her with a ceremonious gesture in front of my father, who would take her beak in his left hand and her arched tail in his right and lift her ceiling-wards to the full extent of his arms. In the nest beneath, and wrapped in a napkin, lay a queenly clutch of boiled brown eggs.

It is strange that a bird so conspicuous and endearing as the yellow-hammer has not attracted more notice from the poets. Some amends have been made by those two kindred and observant spirits, one in the last century and one in this; John Clare and Edmund Blunden; and Andrew Young wrote some typical lines describing how he acted as shepherd to a 'golden flock'. One of Blunden's earliest poems, dated 1916, happily catches the 'rural admixture of shrill and sweet' in the song and the gaiety and verve of the singer, who 'gives the sun a cheer'. Both must have brought him solace in that dark time, with doubtless a twinge of the homesickness that the bird aroused in Robert Nichols, writing under the same ordeal. Hudson, describing in *Birds and Man* a rainy pilgrimage to Selbourne in 1896, quotes from a poem by Faber:

> *And there he is within the rain,*
> *And beats and beats his tune again,*
> *Quite happy in himself.*

Clare fixes the image of the bird brilliantly in his phrase, 'with yellow breast and head of solid gold'; but it is the nest of dry grass, with its lining of 'the horse's sable hair', and the fascination of 'the pen-scribbled eggs' which have a particular charm for him, whether the nest be hidden beneath a tall spear thistle or a tuft of rank grass, near enough for the brooding hen to hear the song of her mate, who makes of 'that old molehill' a Parnassus. In his old age, an exile in Northampton asylum, the poet recalls the bird and its nest as one of the happy associations of his youthful, hopeless love for Mary Joyce:

> *There's the yellowhammer's nest, bonny Mary O!*
> *Where she hides her golden breast, bonny Mary O!*
> *On her mystic eggs she dwells, with strange writing on their shells,*
> *Hid in the mossy grass, Bonny Mary O!*

To the hieroglyphics on the egg the bird owes its other name of the scribbling, or writing lark. As children we had difficulty in finding their nests, but when we succeeded I remember looking at the 'mystic' eggs in awe. Did they spell out the words of an incantation, which, if deciphered correctly and murmured with shut eyes, would conjure up a genie? Or again, might not the signs resolve into an 'Open Sesame' – the password to be spoken at the gates of Babylon? Yet surely the most plausible interpretation is that of the old country folk, who declare that the bird itself has scrawled on the eggs the injunction, "Don't 'ee steal my eggs.'

Shortly before his death I happened in conversation with an old friend, for whom the yellow-hammer had been a lifelong favourite, to refer to it as Gladdy. He was delighted with the name, saying that it precisely expressed the feelings that the bird and its song aroused in him. He himself thought of it as a Benedicite bird and was sure its song was an exhortation: 'Be thankful-and-go-down-on-your . . . *knees!*'

His version of the song recalled an incident that had occurred a year or two before in North Devon. An old cottage in the hamlet where I was staying had been bought by a lady from the suburbs as a holiday *pied-à-terre*. She had thoroughly modernised it and would show it proudly to all comers. One summer afternoon, when I was passing the gate, I heard her call my name. She appeared to be in some distress. 'Do you see that man?' she asked, pointing down the road to a figure walking slowly away. 'He has just been here in my cottage. Forgive me, I am a little upset. Oh, it was nothing unpleasant, nothing nasty, but uncomfortable and . . . and sad.' There were tears in her eyes.

It seemed that she had been having a nap in the sitting-room, which opened straight into the little front garden, when a slight noise woke her and she saw a man standing in the doorway. She took him for a tramp at first and told him to go away; but he pleaded with her to let him come in for a few moments and she had not the heart to refuse. He was well over seventy, she thought, shabbily but neatly dressed; and feeling that he had an honest face, she offered him a seat by the fire-place. He was tired from his walk and sat in silence with his head bowed. After some minutes she asked if she could get him something to drink: he nodded and thanked her, and she went into the kitchen to fetch a glass of milk. When she returned, he was on his knees, his eyes closed and his lips moving. She stepped quickly back into the kitchen and waited. Then, hearing him get up, she returned to the sitting-room and handed him the glass; he drank the milk down in a gulp or two.

The silence continued and she began to wonder how she could get rid of him. At last she asked him if there was anything more he wanted. He shook his head, thanked her, and moved towards the door. There he bowed and told her that he had been born and bred in that very cottage and that when he was still a youngster he had run away to sea. His life had been hard and he had never thought to come back; but finding himself in Bideford he made up his mind to walk out to see the old home and say a prayer in it once more before he died. She had followed him to the gate and was watching him set off on his long walk back as I came up.

'I wasn't a bit frightened,' she continued. 'At first I just resented his intrusion. But the curious thing is that now' – and the tears came back into her eyes – 'now, I am the one who seems to be the intruder.'

Then she pointed to the hedge where a yellowhammer was singing.

'You know about birds, don't you?' she said. 'Just as the old man got to the gate, he made such a funny remark and it was the only time he smiled. He looked at me and pointed to the bird and said, "Ah, Mum, my life has been pretty much what that birdie there says: A little bit of bread and no cheese! But I'm thankful for what the good Lord has been able to spare." I can't think what he can have meant, can you? And what is the bird's name?'

I told her, and added that the people round about called it Gladdy.

THE WHITE GATE

eing the portal or barbican of our domain, the White Gate achieved as the years went by a sort of Delphic eminence. It would listen to appeals or confidences, echo to laughter, or stand by in reproof – as when my elder sister turned on the tap of the milk-float and neither of us could turn it off. White as the Gate itself, the tide hissed and spluttered among the dust and stones until our screams brought an enraged milkman to stem the flow and there fell about our heads a scolding to end all scoldings. Our mother, who always seemed to have to do the dirty work where punishment was deserved, for once cajoled our father into administering a rebuke – a rebuke more dreadful for its rarity.

The Gate was at once a beginning and an end, a point of arrival and departure, a gesture of welcome and farewell. When we went off to school the entire household had to go down to the White Gate to wave us off, and as the station taxi bore us away along the Avenue we would watch through tears the group of gesticulating figures merge into a white blur until the corner at the end was turned and they were lost to sight. Equally, we would gather there to greet a welcome visitor – we hid if the visitor was a stranger or not *persona grata* – waving wildly as the carriage or car passed, and then rush up the drive behind it to be ready at the front door as the visitors got out.

I think especially of Saturday afternoons, waiting at the White Gate for my father's return from the City – for, dutiful breadwinner that he was, he went to his office on most Saturdays. He would walk home from the station by way of the main road, the canal towing-path and the semi-private drive to the Hall into which the Avenue led. He had a singularly powerful whistle: *tu-whee*, or *tu-tu-whee*, like a curlew's; and before his tall figure strode into sight we would hear the whistle shrilling across the fields. Our dog Pincher would hear it first, and give a whine and break into a run. Often dashing through the hedge and across open country, he easily outstripped us however hard we scampered towards the enveloping hug.

One September morning, when my brother and I had gone down to the White Gate to see him off – for he seldom failed to walk to the station and was vexed when the weather was rainy and a taxi had to be called – we lingered watching him go. Just before he turned the corner at the end of the Avenue, we heard his whistle and saw him pointing with his stick: a heron was flying low over the fields, head bent back, legs trailing almost horizontally behind, and the great grey wings flapping nearly low enough to brush the tree-tops. There was nothing very odd about this, for herons were common enough round Pipers Hill; it was just that he knew, and we knew, that we all shared the joy of seeing one, so we waved back as hard as we could to show that we had received his message, and he responded with a wave and another whistle. But the incident has proved memorable as the immediate forerunner of another more noteworthy.

My brother and I must have made our ways separately back to the house because, having occupied myself with this and that for some little time, I found myself alone in the hall when the telephone rang. I hated answering the telephone – the squeaky, cracked voices at the other end were unintelligible to me and I felt a fool when I kept having to apologise for not understanding – and so I waited for someone else to come; but no one did, and the ringing seemed to grow more and more peremptory. At last, I plucked up my courage, took off the receiver and, remembering to press the lever which in those days was essential if the caller was to be heard, stammered out our number. The croaky voice proved, thank Heaven, to be my father's. 'That's you, Bosh, is it? That's a surprise! I'm at the station. The train is due, so I haven't a moment to lose. You know the barn at the bridge by the boat-house? Well, on the side facing the canal there's a big grey moth. I think it's a red underwing. It might be there if you run like hares. There's the whistle! Good luck!' There was a click and silence. I put back the receiver, almost as excited at having heard everything he said – I became quite good at answering after that – as at the report he had given. I shouted for my brother and gave him the message, and he quickly collected his net and 'smelling-bottle' and together we did run as fast as we could to the barn. We could hardly believe our luck, for there, set off strongly against the black boards, was a beautiful tabby-winged shape in the form of a triangle with rounded corners. My brother had to stretch to reach it and as it fluttered into the net, we could see through the gauze the velvety crimson and black of the lower wings; and on closer examination each upper wing appeared to have two dark-pencilled eyes, one round and startled, the other a narrow slit like that of the oriental arch-villain of my youth, Dr Fu Manchu. It became one of the most treasured specimens in his collection; and that evening my father's excitement, hardly less than our own, had the added zest of satisfaction that he had correctly identified the moth! As usual, he at once shortened the name and ever afterwards this species was referred to as a 're-dunder'.

That first meeting with an actual 're-dunder' was the more fascinating for me because, when I was much smaller, I had impersonated one in a production of *A Midsummer Night's Dream* in a local rose-garden! I had been cast for the non-speaking part of Moth and my mother, seeking inspiration for my costume in South's book, had chosen the red underwing as her model. I was dressed in a short, brownish-grey tunic with long sleeves, which, when my arms were at my sides, cunningly concealed the pieces of bright crimson material sewn with big crescents of – I like to think – black velvet that represented the lower wings. Except for my antennae, made of gold picture-wire fixed to an elastic headband, I was an inconspicuous figure; but when with the other fairies I mounted guard over the sleeping Titania, I was told I must raise my arms to shoulder height so that the full effect of my beautiful under wings might burst upon the audience. I remembered to do as I was bid and felt that all eyes must be on me; yet I am sure, on reflection, that I was quite outshone by my elder sister, whose glorious red-gold hair shining above her bright green dress was the loveliest Mustard Seed imaginable.

It is a long time since I last saw a 're-dunder' (whither have they fled?). But the passage of time seems to sharpen old memories and in my mind's eye there is an image of a grey triangle on black boarding that has outlasted reality. If the moths that we later saw there have departed, so has the barn itself: a new road has smothered it.

THE WILD PATCH

he Wild Patch, delightful in its gentle wildness, was a favourite part of the garden with all of us. It measured about a quarter of an acre and was, as I have mentioned, a piece of rough ground planted in agreeable disorder with shrubs and trees. On summer evenings my father, returning tired from the City, loved to stroll to and fro along the paths that encircled it – each autumn my mother planted it with new groups of daffodils and narcissi – and we children, the dog and the cats made endless use of it for hunting or hiding. In the Spring, first the crocuses and then the daffodils took the stage, running hither and thither as they willed, like dancers bearing tapers. The trees – two or three oaks and beeches, a rowan and a whitebeam – could hardly have been planted more than twenty years before we ran and rolled and hid beneath them, for their trunks were slender and their bark not yet deeply grooved. The shrubs grew closer together at the far end; laurel, currant, broom, weigela – we didn't call it that, but 'Australian honeysuckle' – and philadelphus – we didn't call it that either, but 'syringa' – and delicious was the smell of strawberries and cream that poured from the syringa's frothing blossoms. This shrubby part of the Wild Patch was darker, more shadowy, more mysterious than the rest, with a hint of witchery in it, whereas the more open part near the centre and western end of the Garden had broader, sunnier spaces and seemed to borrow colour from my mother's herbaceous border close by.

At this sunny end there was one tree which I regarded with a mixture of affection and awe. This was an almond tree. It had a beautifully polished trunk, the colour of mahogany, smooth as satin to the touch of a finger-tip, and in a breeze the slender leaves were themselves like fingers running up and down the strings of a harp. In Spring it was one of the marvels of the year. As one by one the blossoms came out among the naked branches, each like a whorl of pink icing on a birthday cake, and went scrambling up in their hundreds and thousands towards the blue of the sky, or came sliding down over the green of the grass and the brown of the earth, I felt it must all taste as sweet as it looked – yet only the early bees knew how to reach its secret hoards of sweetness.

If the garden was, as indeed it still is, the Garden of Eden of my imagining, the almond tree was The Tree of the Knowledge of Good and Evil, for all that it bore in autumn little silver-furred nuts instead of tempting golden apples. Beside it, quite plain in my mind's eye, stood Adam and Eve, in aprons stitched with laurel leaves (for I did not know what fig leaves looked like, there being no fig-tree in our garden), motionless and aghast at the sound of the Voice of God in the garden in the cool of the evening. It was from that darksome part of the Wild Patch where the shrubs congregated that the Voice came; and since it was no easier then than it is now to picture God Himself, I accepted the literal meaning of the words and imagined a disembodied Voice approaching through the shadows, a presence to be feared and wondered at, but featureless; and as it came nearer and nearer I could sense how fearfully Adam and Eve trembled and catch the slithering sound of the Serpent as it slid away into the familiar flowers of the herbaceous border, where it listened to the stern pronouncement, a glint of defiance in its steely eyes. Then how terrible it was to picture the Angel driving the guilty pair to the White Gate and standing there with the flaming sword lifted high above them as they trudged in tears out of the Garden, when for once the double leaves of the Gate crashed together and the iron bolt was rammed down! What of the Tree of Life? The Book of Genesis is reticent about its appearance and position, so I gave it no counterpart in our garden. But I sometimes wondered whether it might not have been the solitary oak-tree, two hundred yards away out there in the water-meadows, transplanted thither to be out of reach, but near enough to act as a warning.

In the centre of the Wild Patch I had my own tree – not that I would have tried to prevent my brother and sisters from climbing it had they been so disposed. But I felt it to be mine because it was I who discovered how climbable it was, and I enjoyed the climb into the enveloping greenery on branches that were almost as regular as the rungs of a ladder. I sometimes took a book up with me, but seldom read it for long, for in the comfortable seat that I found for myself a yard or so from the top, I would lean against the pliant trunk and encourage it to swing me this way and that. The motion was so gentle and beguiling that even the pleasure of reading fell into second place and I would give myself up to the pure contentment of listening to the rustle of the leaves and watching how their sunlit shapes dissolved and reformed among their own shadows. And I would look up to the sky, which now seemed so close, and felt how much I should like to sail among the cloud archipelagos, whose spits and bars and dunes, islands and promontories appeared and disappeared in the tides of blue.

Once, a heron swung over on its great wings, its long legs dangling so low that I almost ducked; and another time a turtle-dove, one of the loveliest of all our summer visitors, came looping down and perched on the neighbouring beech; I felt almost reproachful that it had not chosen my oak. From there it began to purr, as only a turtle-dove can, and in all my life, however many times I may have listened in gratitude to its soothing tones, the singer and its listener have never been so close to each other as they were that summer afternoon on their neighbouring perches of oak and beech.

A bird's voice may become a favourite, less through any intrinsic excellence than because of some peculiar harmony between the sound and its environment. On fine afternoons in high summer, such as warmed me on my oak-top, no sound more exactly suits the pervasive languor and motionless array of sunlight and shadow than the purring call of the turtle-dove as it throbs above fields newly mown. It is as if Summer herself had fallen asleep beneath the trees and one could hear her quiet breathing. The call boasts no melody in the true sense, no cadence, no variation, yet has an intensity and a resonance that are rather felt than heard; it seems to stroke the air and the back of the listener's neck. Virgil knew the bird well and regarded its voice as an inseparable accompaniment to summer days in the country. Whereas to him it seemed to 'moan from the soaring elm', I have never felt its mood to be other than that of contentment; and I feel it to be so whenever I hear it – now, alas, so rarely. The singer may plead or lament for a space, yet always with an underlying confidence of success at last; or, if separation is to be the lovers' lot, the notes proclaim the constancy of love which finds words in the old Dorset folk-song, 'The Turtle Dove':

> *Yet I will love but thee alone,*
> *Till the streams run from the seas, my dear,*
> *Till the streams run from the seas.*

It is doubtless foolish to attribute human emotions to a bird or any other animal, yet on a summer afternoon the folly may be condoned in a listener who looks through half-closed eyes at the rafts of elder bloom afloat above a garden wall or, half dreaming, is back again in childhood swinging on the branch of an oak-tree.

The turtle-dove, which the French so musically call *tourterelle*,* comes late to our islands in summer, and there is a particular joy in seeing it for the first

---

*Its upstart cousin, almost its supplanter in recent years, the collared dove, is not a favourite of mine, with its inanely repetitive call and occasional little snarls.

time, its arrowy, limber shape swinging down through the trees or over the brow of a hill, with an unmistakeable lilt in the beat of its wings and the light catching the crescent of white spangles on the tail.

The nest, which we often found in the taller and more ragged hedges round Pipers Hill, is a model of economy, little more than a raft of twigs delicately but firmly interwoven, yet so diaphanous that the two slender white eggs lying in it can be seen from below: I recall how fascinated I used to be by the glow of the fresh yolks inside the shells. The most beautiful nest I have ever found was in a hawthorn tree in full bloom on the slope of a chalk down in Dorset, for which the eggs in their light hammock among the crowding white blossoms formed a perfect, almost mystical centre-piece. The discovery had a memorable sequel. One winter's evening, many years later, but a while ago now, when a chilly rain rapped the windows of my suburban railway-carriage on the way back from a weary day in London, some unaccountable turn of the wheel of consciousness threw me a vision of the nest among the may-bloom. The scent of the flowers, the burden of the insects and the gleaming shells of the eggs were vividly apparent, and I began to picture how, when the bird returned to brood, the sunlight would burnish her head and breast and the moonlight turn them to silver. I seemed to be in two places: my spirit in that ivory bower, my body rattling on.

VISITORS TO THE WILD PATCH

rowsily swinging in my oak-tree one afternoon I became aware that other and smaller wings were waving above my head, that a different shadow had danced in amongst those of the leaves. My caller was a butterfly with its attendant shadow, and almost at once both came to rest on a sunlit leaf only a foot or two from my hand. The butterfly stayed a moment motionless with closed wings, then opened and closed and opened them again, the shadows they threw on the bright surface of the leaf making answer to each motion. Now the wings were spread wide and the little creature settled down to bask in the warmth. Though surprised at it climbing so high, I knew at once what it was, for we always saw numbers of its tribe in the lanes of North Devon, when my father had told us that they were called 'Speckled Wood or Wood Argus'; and, as was his wont, he had endeared it to us with his own dimunitive, 'Wood Argie' (hard 'G'). The butterfly I was looking at was so close that I could see the sunshine lighting up each hair in the warm brown furry parts where the ringed and dappled wings are joined to the body, and glinting on the white dots at the ends of the antennae; and I could look right into the mimic argus eyes on the forewings, so black and yet so sparkling, with no hint of warning (to me at any rate), no intention, as I fancied, but to answer my look with a smile. 'Wood Argie' is indeed one of the tamest and most friendly of all butterflies, the close companion of any walk along a shady lane, where the chequer-work of sunlight and shadow finds a replica among the darks and lights of the brown and golden wings. In recent years, when some malign influence seems to have banished so many butterflies from our fields and hedges, the numbers of this modest species have grown no less. It has two broods, so it may emerge early enough in the year to keep company with the last of the hazel catkins and will still be taking one of its leisurely saunters when the nuts are ripe.

A small bird that came each year in springtime to nest in the Wild Patch was the willow warbler. The nest is extremely difficult to find, being hidden beneath a tuft of grass or low-growing plant, well protected by arching stems or bramble sprays; but when found, its small oven shape, as John Clare describes it, of moss interwoven with grass and root fibres, gives great delight. To look in through the hole in the side, you have to go down on your knees, and from that angle its feather-lined cup has an irresistibly snug and cosy look, and you can see lying among the crowded feathers what appears to be a countless abundance of tiny speckled eggs – probably not more than six or eight. I think I must be allowed to quote several lines from Clare here:

> *Built like an oven, through a little hole,*
> *Scarcely admitting e'en two fingers in,*
> *Hard to discern, the bird's snug entrance win.*
> *'Tis lined with feathers warm as silken stole,*
> *Softer than seats of down for painless ease,*
> *And full of eggs scarce bigger even than peas!*
> *Here's one most delicate, with spots as small*
> *As dust and of a faint and pinky red.*

The willow warbler has a most beautiful song – a song so conspicuous and persistent at nesting time to anyone familiar with it that it is surprising that many people in the course of a country walk can pass a succession of singing willow warblers without apparently hearing them. The treble song wanders in shallow ripples through a descending scale until it trickles away into silence. Yes, the song has 'a dying fall', but fortunately the bird is always ready to perform 'that strain again'. Viscount Grey of Falloden, in his ever-delightful book *The Charm of Birds*, calls the singer 'the everlasting bird'; and I remember myself spending a whole hour one morning in the Wild Patch counting the drifts of song and noting that they were repeated on an average every fifteen seconds. (Can I have listened to 240 drifts in succession? I have little doubt that I did). W.H. Hudson devotes some eloquent passages to the song in *Birds and Man*, noting something human-like in the quality of the voice, its timbre. It is a song which seems to wave goodbye to Winter; it has a smile in it reminiscent of the reflection of sunlit water on the trunks of trees along a river bank; and each year, when the bird is due, my ears grow alert for the first chime, which always precedes the sight of the greenish slip of a figure darting among the catkins of birch or hazel..

The lines from Clare that I have quoted come from his poem 'The Pettichap's Nest', the title giving rise to a little conundrum. The name petti-chaps certainly applies to one of the summer visitors to our islands known as *Sylviidae*, a designation pleasantly evocative of green shades and their 'green

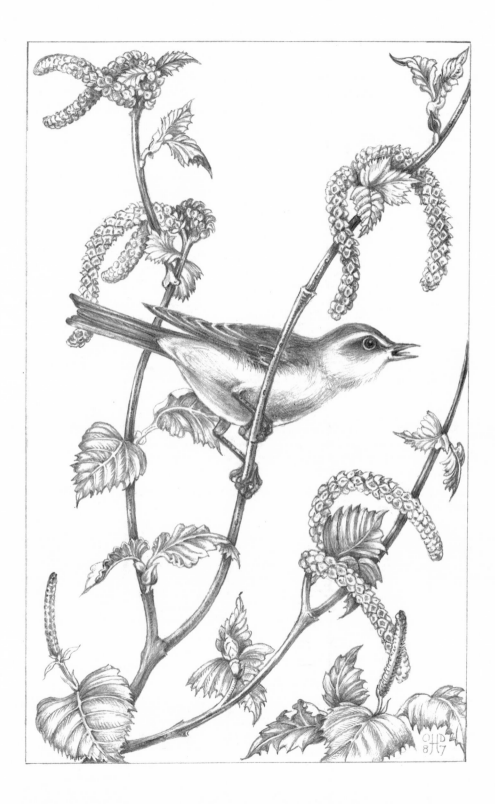

thoughts'. But there precision ends. The *Oxford Dictionary* applies the term to the garden warbler (and even to the long-tailed tit), but admits that it has been applied to other members of the family; and since they are all small fellows and have in consequence small cheeks the name itself gives no aid to definition – unless one regards it as onomatopaeic, when it may be taken as echoing the little pulsating song of the chiffchaff that seems to tick out the passage of time during the longer days. Certainly the chiffchaff's song, as the accepted name for the bird denotes, is most often a disyllable, yet it has sometimes to my ear (now grown almost too gross to hear it at all!) a hint of syncopation which would justify the light middle syllable: indeed Clare remarks of the pettichap (he makes it singular) in the journal he kept in 1824-5, 'that its note is more like "chippachap".' But, you see, he is inconsistent, because his poem clearly describes the willow warbler's nest, which is placed on the ground, whereas the chiffchaff's is always at least a foot or two above it, and the spots on the eggs are dark chocolate in colour, not 'a faint and pinky red'. Gilbert White makes one reference in his *Natural History of Selborne* to the pettichaps (in the plural) which merely adds to the puzzle. He speaks of a rare little bird resembling a whitethroat, yet with a more white and silvery breast, and tells how it 'runs up and down the stems of the crown imperials, and, putting its head into the bells of those flowers sips the liquor which starts in the nectarium of each petal.' What can this have been, since surely neither the willow warbler nor the chiffchaff were 'rare' at Selborne? And the other claimants to the title, the garden warbler and the wood warbler, sing totally different songs! Clearly opinions differ and I must be excused for committing myself. When all is said, the problem is of trifling account in the scale of our indebtedness to the birds themselves for there is no day so fine and no spot so fair but is made to seem finer and fairer by the presence of one or other of these silver-tongued dryads.

AT HOME IN THE WILD PATCH

ot far from my oak-tree my elder sister and I made what we called at first our 'tree-house' and later on our 'country residence'; but it was not, like Wendy's, perched high above the ground among branches, but based on solid earth, with a floor of tussocks of grass and leaves fallen from the over-spreading beech. We drove some stakes into the ground and filled the spaces between with turves and moss and twigs of every shape, and hung an old sack over the doorway. We felt like cave-dwellers. We were careful to choose a spot where we believed our mother had not planted any daffodils, but before we had finished building they had come tripping round from all sides right up to the walls, and one or two had popped up through the 'floor' inside. In the summer there was nothing on the floor but acorn cups and beech mast and dead leaves scampered over by agile spiders. No one was allowed in except on special request or without a respectful tap on one of the doorposts.

It was not long before we found we had a lodger. One afternoon when we were lying half asleep in the shadowy interior, a small brown bird came in – without knocking – and flew to a dark corner behind our heads: it looked like a flying mouse, but instead of a long, dangling, twisty tail it appeared to have hardly a tail at all.

'It isn't a bat, is it?' whispered my sister in alarm, trying in vain to cover her brush of red hair with her hands.

'Ssh, it's a wren,' I whispered back. 'Keep quite still, it may have a nest.' Disregarding my own instructions, I turned and raised my head towards the dark corner. There was a sort of pop and a small round object whizzed past my head, skimming my sister's, and shot out through a gap in the sacking door. Directly afterwards, there was a loud burst of song, like the spurt of flame from a lighted match. Relieved that the visitor was not a bat, my sister asked:

'Do you really think it has a nest?'

I did, and it had, for there in the dark corner among the dead leaves and sticks, I could see a ball of moss and grass, with a hole in the side, round and black like a Cyclops eye. It was not a menacing but an inviting eye, and I could not forbear to crook my forefinger and feel inside. The nest was empty – and how the wren could have made it so quickly and without our noticing we could not imagine.

On the next two or three days we – very unwisely – crooked our fingers through the hole but never felt anything inside but moss. Once, as we crawled through the sacking door, a wren whizzed out, raising our hopes that the next time we tried there would be an egg: but no, always the dull old moss! Then one day when we were carrying out some necessary repairs to the outside, my sister let out a gasp and pointed. There, just below her finger-tip, was another ball of moss and grass, with another round 'eye' in the side, but sticking out over its lower lid was the tip of a feather. In went a curved finger and this time it touched eggs, smooth and warm, and when we peered in we could see their white shells speckled with sandy red. The little hen cave-dweller (for it has always amused me that Linnaeus gave the wren the Latin name *Troglodytes troglodytes* – double-dyed too!) had on this occasion rejected her mate's first choice of a nesting site in the shadows and had preferred his second, in the light. Thereafter, for a day or two before school claimed us with its relentless clutch, we would listen to the cock's outburst of song and, when we could catch sight of him, watch how his upright chequered tail would almost swivel on its base with the fervour of his joy or pride.

A wren's song never fails to surprise by its vehemence. Yet as often as I have heard it, in copse or hedgerow, among barns and woodstacks, or in the familiar surroundings of my own house and garden, it is not to domestic scenes that my mind is apt to spring back, but to one of two wild mountainsides far removed from each other and from home. First, I see a gulch high up among the desolate hills of South Uist in the Outer Hebrides, where a burn slips down ledge after ledge in little cascades of silver, leaving each time an ale-coloured pool at whose margins grow foxgloves and ragged robins and meadowsweet so little to be expected in this wild spot; and suddenly from a recess overhung with ferns there comes a wren's burst of song, cool, clear and ringing. Again, another remembered song rings out, piercing the weird stillness along the stoney shore of Lough Ouler lying in the pouch of that monstrous marsupial Tonelagee in the Wicklow Mountains. Once more I see the heart-shaped face of the water, one half furrowed by a thousand waves, the other flat and motionless and black as ebony.

Wordsworth never forgot the impact of a wren's song heard in an unlikely place:

At Home in the Wild Patch

Our steeds remounted and the summons given,
With whip and spur we through the chauntry flew
In uncouth race, and left the cross-legged knight,
And the stone-abbot, and that single wren
Which one day sang so sweetly in the nave
Of the old church, that – though from recent showers
The earth was comfortless, and touched by faint
Internal breezes, sobbings of the place
And respirations, from the roofless walls
The shuddering ivy dripped large drops – yet still
So sweetly mid the gloom the invisible bird
Sang to herself, that there I could have made
My dwelling-place, and lived for ever there
To hear such music.

Even as I write now, half a century and more later, a wren's song from an apple tree outside my window throws me on its jet of notes these images of the past – if indeed moments intensely felt and gratefully apprehended can ever pass. I would call them part of the poetry, part of the music of life, which in our anxious hours and fretful ways we must heed lest our spirits starve. Such are the moments when, the bird's song being as it seems an act of praise and my own response to it another, the blending of the two have brought me as close as I can get to the presence and personality of the Creator. Perhaps I should not venture to speak for the bird, since doubtless its own joy, needing no association with mine, is sufficient of itself.

CYCLAMEN, NEAR AND FAR

 few feet from the almond tree I have spoken of my mother had made a small rockery. It was hardly more than a mound embossed with a few big stones and weathered bricks, over and around which clustered such familiar plants as aubretia, yellow and white alyssum, arabis, dwarf phlox, Granny's pinks and rock-roses of various colours. It would have excited little or no interest in a connoisseur of alpines, but in the flowering season it was pretty enough, especially in April when the smaller kinds of bulb thrust up their modest flowers, so shapely in line and pure in colour: angel's tears, dog's-tooth violets, scyllas and miniature daffodils with their hooped and golden petticoats. In Autumn, when the flowers had faded and the green of the leaves was drab, there was just one corner where the season worked a small miracle. A flower of the tenderest pink, then another and then another, would shoulder its way up through the bare earth, on stems far too tender, it seemed, for so tough a task, the delicately voluted petals making one think of the ears of small animals, or the rosy fan-shells we used to find on the shores of North Devon bays, or again of the coral necklaces my sisters wore at parties.

Now, in old age, if I were so foolish as to attempt the invidious task of naming my 'top ten' favourites among flowers, the little autumn-flowering cyclamen would certainly find a place, not merely for its intrinsic beauty, or for the recollection of its annual renewal of delight in the garden of early childhood, but because of certain passages or moments in my life which have attached themselves to this fragile flower or to which it has imparted a poetic overtone.

As we grow older, things do, I think, touch us for their associations hardly less than for themselves – especially for some reason, flowers. Long after I had grown up – and indeed I had already passed my half-century – I had an unexpected encounter with a cyclamen in a London art gallery near

St James's Square which specialised in paintings of the great seventeenth-century Dutch School. The flower on that occasion was only its painted likeness, but it set in motion there and then two curiously vivid reveries. The artist had set the flower at the front of his jewel-bright bouquet and had painted both it and its marbled leaf with an exquisite feeling for their form and colour. The bent head brought to my mind, as it continues to do in life, Keats' 'carved angels, ever eager-eyed . . . with hair blown back'; and the leaf had just those 'ghost signatures' that we used to make in childhood by folding a piece of paper, opening it, writing our names with a full pen along the crease and then folding it again, so that the ink smudged and slithered about to make strange ribs and vertebrae.

As I scrutinised this Dutch likeness of a Botticellian flower, the associative magic began to work, and my thoughts skimmed away in time and place to an eventful episode in my not very eventful adult life. A few days after 'Munich' I found myself, *mirabile dictu*, having tea with the King and Queen of Italy at San Rossore, their country home near Pisa. It was indeed a sort of discovery, for I did not move, nor have I habitually moved, in such circles, and as the youngest and most negligible member of a delegation to Italy, I stood at the edge of the gathering, incredulous yet fascinated at the odd hap of my workaday self being part of it.

I did not at first notice the cyclamen. The Queen (and how beautiful and stately she was in her night-blue dress!) had been talking of the clinics she had helped to found for victims of encephalitis; and the diminutive King, after sending a footman to fetch a macintosh cape blotched with green and yellow, had been describing with loud laughter – while the upturned points of his grey moustache shuttled up and down the grooves declining on either side of his nose – how he had converted its former warlike purpose of concealing an officer in the tank corps to the more peaceful expedient of hoodwinking the pheasants on his estate. 'You see, my English friends,' His Majesty went on, 'you see that sport plays some part in our lives here;' and pointing to the old English sporting prints which hung on the green-and-silver striped walls, he recalled that he had bought them with the house from the Grand Duke of Tuscany. Their titles, 'Bringing 'em in', 'View Halloo', and so on, seemed to exhale a whiff of common day and blow it about the glittering glass and porcelain, the rainbow-hued stalactites of the chandelier, the swords and spurs and braided uniforms of the assembled company, and in and out among the unimaginable cates that loaded the long table down the middle of the room. I thought of Porphyro's banquet and murmured to myself:

> *With jellies soother than the creamy curd*
> *And lucent syrops, tinct with cinnamon.*

Suddenly I became aware of the cyclamen: how could I not have noticed them sooner? They were heaped in three silver épergnes at the centre and either end of the table – great pyramids of glowing rose, which in their brilliance and purity abashed all the other colours in the room. The day before we had seen hosts of them growing wild on the Asiago Plateau, embroidering the copses and meadows where clouded yellow butterflies were on the wing, and sending 'their light of laughing flowers' over the very graves of British soldiers fallen in the campaign of 1918 – those graves that we had come to honour. Wherever we had gone, people had gathered in the piazzas of the little towns to greet us with cries of *'Pace! Pace!'*, a load of fear just lifted from their hearts. It seemed as if these spring-like flowers were breaking into bloom to confirm the assurance, to proclaim the renewal, of hope. Yet here, I thought, in a palace, they were merely a part – albeit the loveliest and most magical part – of the prevailing fantasy! At that moment, a gilt clock beneath a glass dome at the farther end of the room began to chime. I glanced at my watch (for train departures and errant baggage still haunted the fringes of my mind) and saw that the time was a quarter to four. But the gilt clock knew otherwise and went on in plangent tones to strike affirmatively – thirteen. If the entire assembly had sprouted wings and flown to the top of the Leaning Tower it would have been but the order of that day . . .

The gallery, I remember, was rather hot, and I gave a slight gasp and looked again at the painting in front of me. The flower appeared innocent of any motive other than to be its pretty painted self; but the leaf? Or was the flower in collusion? This time I was transported back to England, but further off in years. I found myself standing outside the school gate after Sunday morning chapel with a friend, an Indian (or, as he would now be called, a Pakistani) and we were waiting for the car that was to take us a little distance into the country to spend the afternoon with an elderly lady, the widow of a General, both of whom had known my friend's father for many years.

Presently a blue Daimler, with long, low bonnet and deeply corrugated radiator, draws up; the chauffeur jumps out, shakes hands with my friend, and opens the door at the back for us to climb in. He returns to the wheel, and away we go, sidling and swaying on the grey corded cushions to the leonine purr of the engine. My friend detaches the speaking-tube from its hook and calls: 'Are they all well at the Manor, Glide?' The chauffeur can be seen lifting his head to the mouthpiece and the crackly tones come back: 'Very well, thanking you kindly, Master Mahmud. And may I hen-quire if you have good news from Dehra Dun?' This exchange is no more than a piece of ritual to prove that the apparatus works. For my friend at once leans forward and pulls aside the intervening window so that conversation henceforward may run on more sociable lines.

It is one of those warm days that almost invariably come at the beginning of the Michaelmas term to make games of rugger an anomaly; when swallows fall uneasily into rank on telephone wires, when garden flowers are so bright that they seem to give out heat as well as colour, and the blackberries in the hedges have the dark glitter of birds' eyes. A dissertation from Glide on horsepower is interrupted by a joint ejaculation from the two of us at the back: 'Look, there's a clouded yellow! We must stop.' To which Glide, slowing down, replies: 'You may stop if you wish, Master Mahmud, but if we do I can't answer for your not being late for luncheon.' We drive on – while the butterfly continues to drift across the stubble like a newly fallen elm-leaf. At length we turn off the main road, run down and up between trees, through iron gates and along a short drive to a rambling stone house.

On the look out for us at the front door stands Quickly, who is more of a companion to her mistress than parlourmaid. She runs forward, the light bristling from her spectacles, gives my friend a hug, shakes hands with me and after hurrying us off to wash our hands, waits in the hall to conduct us to the drawing-room. Our hostess rises from a tall chair by the window to greet us. She puts her hands on my friend's shoulders and with a just perceptible tremor of the head leans forward to kiss him on either cheek. Then she takes my hand and invites me to sit in a chair facing her across a low table.

On this table stands a silver bowl full of the beautiful little rosy flowers that used to delight me in my mother's rockery. I am entranced and cannot take my eyes from them. 'You admire my cyclamen, then?' the old lady enquires with disconcerting suddenness. 'They are very lovely to be sure. Roses are my first favourites' – and as my eyes follow the slow wave of her hand I see that there are bowls of them all over the room – 'but the General had a partiality for the little cyclamen: they reminded him of the hill country that he loved. So whenever their season comes round, the roses must yield pride of place to them – just here.' And she puts out her hand to a flat box on the table and draws across a little curtain to reveal through the glass a row of medals, stars and ribbons on a blue velvet lining. 'These were the General's,' she says.

After luncheon – I do not think memory errs in declaring it to have been of roast partridge followed by meringues – my friend whispers that we must go and pay our respects in the kitchen and thank Brook for the delicious fare. 'Not Brook?' I exclaim, as he pushes open the green baize door. 'Not truthfully?' 'What else should the cook's name be?' he answers with a smile, 'seeing that the others are called Quickly and Glide? Besides it rhymes; and you must admit her dishes are poems.' With that he goes dancing off down the stone-flagged passage and knocks on the kitchen door.

The afternoon is spent exploring the sometimes silent, sometimes echoing house right up to the long vaulted attic, now murmurous with the hiss of a slumbering cistern and the buzz of flies gathered against the honey-coloured window-panes. We open a window with a jerk and look over into the churchyard where a jackdaw is waddling among the graves; two more are asleep beside a golden pinnacle of the tower, their heads nodding. Then we go down into the garden, and so quiet is it that we feel we have to tiptoe past the portly apostle yews for fear of disturbing their afternoon nap. We come to the rose garden and beyond to the herbaceous border, where the red admiral and tortoiseshell butterflies are weaving above the constellation of flower heads a ceaseless warp and woof of rustling, flickering wings. My friend gives a sort of groan and, with a look half fierce, half mischievous, says: 'What was that line old Crusoe quoted in form the other day - "England with all thy faults, I love thee still?"' But I have caught sight of an apple-tree with the cyclamen crowding round the bole and am running towards it.

My friend comes up and says: 'I wonder who will inherit this place. It's sad there are no children. But there's a nephew about our age – a very nice chap – whom they were always very fond of. Let's hope he'll get it.' We go on through a wicket gate into the churchyard and he points out the General's grave; there, too, a few cyclamen plants are clustering.

Quickly is hurrying through the rose garden as we return. 'Will you come in now, Master Mahmud?' she says. 'Tea is ready; and you'll remember to wash your hands first, there's good boys.'

This time the picture is quite clear of the quince jelly and home-made milk bread, a *specialité de la maison*. Soon another clock is striking. It is the church clock telling us that the hour is five and it is time to return to school. Our hostess says to Quickly: 'You remembered to do up the bunch of cyclamen, I expect?'

'Yes, madam, and Glide has them in the car.'

Then, turning to me the old lady says: 'I thought you might like them to put in your study. Do not worry,' she continues, seeing me glance at the empty bowl on the table. 'Quickly will pick me some more when you have gone.' At the drawing-room door she gives us each a kiss . . .

I recall once more how hot it had become in the gallery and how at that point I hurried out into the street. It was only a few weeks before that I had heard of my friend's untimely death in India. The Manor House, as it happens, is not far away from my present home and I decided, perhaps rashly, to revisit it as an act of homage to his memory; or at any rate I could go to the church and look through from the churchyard. An opportunity came sooner than I expected. I left the car in the road and glanced up the drive. It was ill kept and there was a general air of neglect; the tops of the apostle yews looked shaggy. Then I remembered hearing that the house had stood empty for some years after the old lady's death and had later been turned, not very successfully, into flats. I walked up a lane between the wall of the garden and a row of overarching beeches to the churchyard. The September sunlight shone warm and bright on the grass, and by contrast the interior of the church was dark and struck chill. Against the south wall of the chancel there was a monument to the General recalling his service under Queen Victoria in Egypt, Matabeleland and South Africa, and under three monarchs in India. On the opposite wall a much newer tablet commemorated an officer whose name was unfamiliar, but the inscription soon made it plain that this was the nephew my friend had spoken of. He had been killed in a brave action during the landings at Anzio in 1944 and was buried in the Beach Head War Cemetery there; and a sentence added that, although he had been born and bred in a different county, he had made the Manor House 'his second home'.

I went out into the churchyard and climbed the slope to the far corner, as I had done long before with my friend. The few patches of cyclamen on the grave had spread and now ran from the angle of the wall for some yards in a thick band of rose. I had not seen so many since the time of that distant pilgrimage to Italy when Peace had seemed, so erroneously, to be reborn. The tall cross bore a brief addition to the original inscription, recording the name of the General's wife and the date of her death: she had just survived the last war. I looked across to the house, where the attic windows peered above the yellow elms (quite soon to catch the plague that made them wither and die), and beyond to the wooded valley and the green hills that folded it in. As if the drift of my musings were in want of an emblem, there came flying from the far end of the churchyard a clouded yellow butterfly on hesitant wings – stopping, side-stepping, lingering among the cyclamen, and gliding on. I watched it slip over the wall and felt it was time to go. Hoping I did not commit an act of sacrilege I stooped and picked two or three cyclamen to put in my buttonhole; and as I retraced my steps to the car I could not help wondering what associations the flower in the old picture might have had for the artist three centuries ago, and whether he had painted it no less for them than for itself.

A CONCATENATION OF CATERPILLARS

peaking of caterpillars,' said my father, as we came to a bend of the River – I suppose we had been discussing the peculiarities of 'sticks' and 'woolly bears' – '*that* is the largest I have ever seen.'

He had stopped; and when he did not speak again, my brother and I, assuming that he was about to tell us of some past monster of his experience, hesitated before demanding, 'What? Where?'

'That, there,' he replied, pointing with his walking-stick. We looked along the length of his whangee to the ferrule, which had lifted the leaf of a succulent plant hung with orange-red flowers.

We gasped. In the green shade, an enormous caterpillar, lost in his own green thoughts, was taking a siesta, his hindquarters clinging to the stem, his fore parts raised and slightly bowed, as if in prayer, and ending abrupt and square-faced in the fashion of a pug or a bull-dog – or even a cobra. Certainly we had seen no larger caterpillar outside *Alice*. It had the colour and plumpness of a well-furnished pea-pod, but on the nether end there was a sort of hook, like the paring of a fingernail, and on what at first seemed to be his forehead were four round eyes, having a dilated pupil edged with a violet iris set against a white crescent of eyeball. All four appeared to glare upward in mingled menace and reproach. As we gazed in speechless wonderment, its jowl began to elongate into a proboscis or trunk that waved from side to side until the round tip of the trunk started to chew the nearest leaf: we could just catch the sound of munching.

'Of course,' exclaimed my father, 'that's what it must be: the caterpillar of an elephant hawk-moth.'

Taking out of his waistcoat pocket the pair of folding scissors he always carried with him, he carefully cut off the stem on which the caterpillar rested and lifted it up for us to take a closer look. Irritated by the interruption of his meal, the caterpillar made two waves of his trunk and then slowly retracted it into the jowl. Our astonishment continued wordless.

'How are we to get it home?' we at last demanded in agony. My father, whose pockets were large and contained an assortment of articles that might be needed on our walks, wore a look of triumph as he took out a round metal box with a perforated lid (of a type familiar to entomologists). But at once his face fell; the box was not nearly large enough to contain our prize.

'There's nothing for it but to put it in one of your hats,' he declared; and so the caterpillar travelled home in a round grey felt of the kind we always used to sport in summer for everyday wear.

The caterpillar appeared unperturbed by the jolting and heat of the journey back and was immediately presented to my mother with a ceremonial flourish and assurances of the delight she would experience on seeing our offering.

'How splendid!' she exclaimed with bravely concealed distaste. 'Wherever did you find it? At least it doesn't look as though it would sting or give you a rash. But all I beg is that you boys don't ask me to look after it when you have gone back to school.'

'Oh, mother, of course not; he will have 'chrysalised' long before that.' This word was our own coinage, much preferred to the pedantic 'pupated': it had a pleasing flavour, reminiscent (though I have never been able to pin down the precise connection) of that Christmas delicacy, crystallised fruits. The caterpillar – not larva, another pedantic word – was placed in an elaborate contraption of inter-connected boxes, muslin and perforated zinc known to us as 'caterpillar-runs', one of the boxes having a layer of earth three or four inches deep.

When the caterpillar had eaten his fill and his beautiful green livery had begun to fade, he burrowed an inch or more into the earth and there made a small cavity in which he wove a barely perceptible cocoon before transforming himself into a dark brown chrysalis. I used to wonder with an agreeable shudder what it might feel like myself to contract into a chrysalis and later expand into something with wings. It might prove to be, in the words of Peter Pan, 'an awfully big adventure.' As we foretold, the caterpillar went to ground before the summer holidays were over; and, sadly, he did not emerge as a moth until we were back at school for the following summer term.

Having as it were, got our eye in, we afterwards found many other elephant hawk caterpillars along the banks of the neighbouring river and canal; they fed on the beautiful orange-flowered balsam (*Impatiens biflora*) that hangs out its intricately carved flowers as did Marvell's oranges, 'like golden lamps in a green night.' Almost more plentiful than the green variety of caterpillar were the brown; these were like small cigars, and against the darker background the painted eyes glittered with an expression sometimes of a snake, sometimes of a spaniel – depending perhaps on the mood of the beholder.

It was not until some years later that we had the chance to see the moths on the wing. There was, as I have remarked earlier, a big rhododendron bush on the upper lawn and at dusk on evenings in late May or early June, when the bush was heaped with bloom, we would wait for the moths to come. It was always at precisely the same time that we would sense in the air a slight whirr, whether by sight or sound it was hard to determine. The first moth had flown in and hung poised on fast-quivering wings, throwing out its proboscis to search for nectar deep in a flower's throat. Another would come and then another – a dozen or more – darting this way and that on wings that even in the dusk had a rosy glow until a prolonged tremor seemed to shake the whole bush; we ourselves almost swirled in the eddies. Then, after five minutes, punctual nearly to the second, the vibrant shapes vanished and stillness returned.

My father, as was his way with all our simple interests, managed to glamorise caterpillars. He shortened the word to 'caterp' with a slight stress on the second syllable, and his exclamation, 'I say, boys, there's a fine caterp!' – for he was usually the first to observe one – lent a tingle of excitement to any discovery.

Writers in neither verse nor prose have done justice to the great army of caterpillars marching in silent regiments through field and forest, heath and hedgerow, resplendent in their panoply of uniform and accoutrement, smooth and hirsute, plumed and tasseled, buttoned, braided and befrogged, their colours proudly flying and lacking only, as I used to lament, the fanfare of trumpets and the roll of drums. 'The very colours of caterpillars,' Isaak Walton agreed, 'are very elegant and beautiful.' The gold-tail, it might be, gorgeous in scarlet and white and bristling with long black hairs as it browses on a hazel leaf; the emperor among the heather, its emerald surcoat studded with bosses of gold; the fox moth, also among the heather, sometimes coiled like a shell, sometimes stretched along a pink flower-head in bars of bronze and gold and black; the ermines and tigers, veritable hussars in busby and bearskin; the grey dagger sprouting from its black velvet tunic cockades of gold and silver; and all the battalions of hoopers and loopers, benders and stretchers in every shade of colour, humped and notched and whelked, pied and striped, spotted, spangled and barred. Whenever now, in my old age, I happen upon one of these valiant campaigners, I hear my father's voice exclaiming, 'Look, boys, there's a fine caterp!'

Our first encounter with one of the most curious of all 'caterps' is fixed in memory. We were playing about on the Lawn one afternoon, when my elder sister let out a shriek and began to run for the house. 'It's a dragon,' she wailed. 'I know it's very small, but it *is* a dragon. Look!' And, a true heroine, she was brave enough to turn in her tracks and point. There, advancing at a brisk and resolute pace, was a weird creature, not exactly breathing fire, but with an undeniable air of menace. It had a broad, elevated front, slimming in a downward curve and rising again to end in a black forked tail, which bent forward over its back. It appeared to be wearing a green hauberk beneath a mantle of deep purple edged with white.

It was my brother, I think, who broke the awed silence with the half-scoffing remark, 'It's only a caterp,' and the rest of us soon felt we could agree with him. South's book was fetched and in it was a plate depicting the creature before us: it was a full-grown caterpillar of the puss moth. One of us ran to get a sprig of willow for it to eat. Its reaction was not of gratitude; no indeed. It still had an astonishing shot in its locker. Vexed by our advances, each of the two prongs in the tail thrust out a pink extension like a finger, which wagged in reproach. We drew back. After a while it condescended to walk onto the willow twig and began to feed. During its meal, we managed to convey it on the twig to the 'run', where very soon afterwards it 'chrysalised', attaching itself to a piece of wood we had provided and spinning a tough cocoon interwoven with pieces of bark.

Isaak Walton had shared our experience three centuries before. He promises his correspondent to 'show you one feeding on a willow-tree – and you shall find him punctually to answer this description: his lips and mouth somewhat yellow; his eyes black as jet; his forehead purple; his feet and hinder parts green; his tail two-forked and black; the whole body stained with a kind of red spores which run along the neck and shoulder blades, not unlike the form of St Andrew's cross, or the letter X, made thus cross-wise, and a white line drawn down his back to his tail; all which add much beauty to his whole body. And it is to me observable, that at a fixed age this caterpillar gives-over to eat; and towards winter, comes to be covered over with a strange shell or crust called an Aurelia; and so lives a kind of dead life, without eating, all the winter.' Again, unhappily, we were not at home to see the moth emerge. This is, to be sure, a magnificent 'cat', soft and furry as a persian, with silver wings delicately veined in filigree patterns of black and grey. My mother, who, even before my father died, never wore coloured dresses, had one made of a light material in a pattern closely resembling the wings, which she spoke of as her 'puss-moth dress' – we used to rag her for pronouncing the word 'mawth'. She wore it at a school prize-giving and I never saw her look more elegant.

Encounters with two other caterpillars have caused me surprise. That strenuous miner-cum-carpenter, the caterpillar of the goat moth, not only bores deeply into trees, its favourite being the willow, but also constructs for

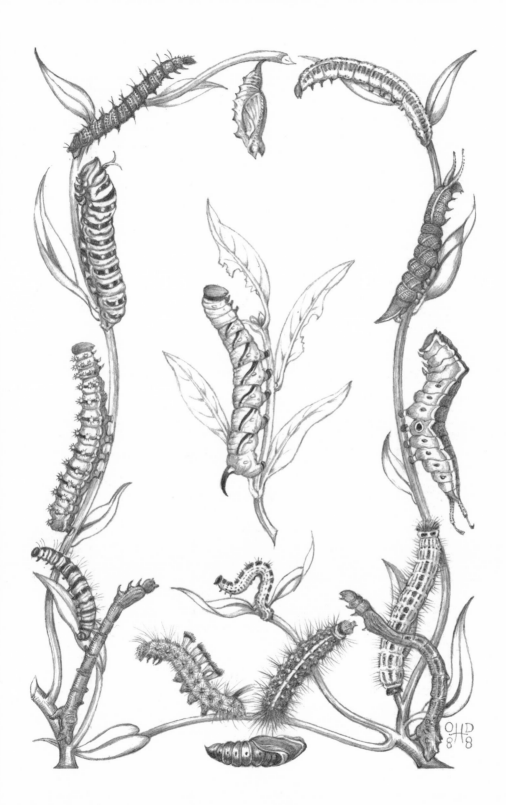

itself out of chips of wood and its own spinnings a remarkably tough 'aurelia', in which having 'chrysalised' it may remain for two or three years in motionless oblivion. The only one of its kind I have ever seen found its way into the house, where it was gathered up and put, not into a 'run', but into a large biscuit tin, which was lined with earth and given a plentiful supply of pieces of rotten wood. It was nearly three inches long, its upper parts dark brown for the whole of its length and its underparts a not very comely shade of fleshy pink: like a dead finger, someone remarked with relish, especially as the creature had about it a smell of mortality – goatish in fact. The next day, to our dismay, it had disappeared, though we felt sure that the lid of the tin, well holed with hammer and nails, had been securely pressed down. Search as we could the caterpillar was nowhere to be found and our nurse was convinced that it would bore through the wardrobe door and devour all our clothes. Two or three days later, when the nursery was being turned out, a rug proved immovable, but at last it yielded to a determined tug. Underneath was the half-metamorphosed caterpillar, which had dug for itself a sort of barrow in the linoleum and in forming a dome had attached to its roof the underside of the rug with a gluey composition of coloured wools, silk and half-chewed fragments of linoleum. It was an impressive work and its destruction, unavoidable as it was, was deeply bewailed. It is sad to recall that for all our solicitude the caterpillar stiffened and dwindled and died.

The other encounter referred to took place many years later on a railway station, and the caterpillar in question made two train journeys with me, to London and back; it was in the days when, to use the accepted word, I 'commuted'. The station was not my usual one – I cannot remember now why I started my journey from there that morning – and while waiting for the train to come in I strolled to the far end of the platform, my thoughts occupied with matters quite other than lepidopteral. At that point, where the stone flags became gravel, a spindly privet bush was growing and from its topmost twig there protruded, like a weather vane, a sumptuous caterpillar which I was not too preoccupied to recognise as that of a privet hawk-moth. I will not try to describe it myself since I could by no means emulate the vivid pen-picture of a Victorian enthusiast writing under the pseudonym 'Acheta Domestica': 'Amongst the most beautifully painted of the caterpillar race are those from which spring the elegant and distinguished tribe of hawk-moths known as Sphinxes, from the form and attitudes of their no less distinguished larvae. None, perhaps, among them are more tastefully decorated than that of the 'privet', with his doublet of the most brilliant apple-green laced by oblique stripes of white and purple, further adorned along the sides by orange-circled spiracles or breathing-holes, and finished at the nether end by a black and yellow horn.'

I had hardly walked round the bush to view its crowning adornment from all angles, when the train came puffing in. Before I knew what I was doing, the old acquisitive larval longings of boyhood overcame me and, hoping I was not observed, I broke off the twig and thrust it and its tenant into my attaché case and got into the train. From what I could see of my companions over the tops of their newspapers I did not think it wise to open the case during the journey, nor was I able myself to concentrate on the morning's news. When I reached my office, the porter found a glass of water for me and in it I stuck the twig and seemingly unruffled caterp, and put it beside my in-tray. Its fame soon spread, and throughout the day it became an object of pilgrimage by my colleagues, some curious, some admiring, some indifferent, some doubting the evidence of their eyes. My secretary was dutifully appreciative, but I noticed that in taking down letters she sat at the far end of the desk and looked up often from her note-book to take a glance sideways to assure herself that it had not crawled in her direction. The journey home was likewise uneventful. My wife, as is her kindly wont, received the offering with no hint of displeasure, and provided a box in which in due course it 'chrysalised'.

One morning the following summer the moth emerged, pale and crumpled, but by the time I got back from the office in the evening the great forewings had expanded to show their habitual colours of seasoned wood, the lower wings resplendent in crimson, cream and black and the long body most nobly barred in matching shades. It was ready to fly. We took it outside and put it on a spray of honeysuckle, where it walked a few uncertain steps. For a moment it stayed motionless; then its wings began to quiver and its body to shake – as an aeroplane does when awaiting the signal to charge along the runway. At no evident signal the moth took off with a whirr that was almost a roar. Springing upward, as we waved farewell, it described a wide circle and returned to execute a flypast which we hoped we might take as a salute. Then it vanished into the dusk and we saw it no more.

THE FIELD: TWO OAK TREES

ll along the eastern side of the garden, and divided from it by a solid wooden fence, lay a field of about seven acres, known in the family as the Field to distinguish it from the other anonymous fields in the immediate neighbourhood. At the house end of the fence there was a gate with a latch and about ten yards beyond the gate grew a large oak. The intervening space formed an additional playground for us, since no matter what crop was being grown in the Field – and it was nearly always grass – the kindly farmer never seemed to mind this particular piece being trampled or rolled on by us or burrowed into by our dog. The dog, a mongrel of dubious parentage – a bull terrier loomed somewhere in his ancestry – made at least two cavernous burrows; we would push a stick into the earth above his buried head and twist it round to make a scratching noise, and this to our delight goaded him to higher and higher pitches of excitement, louder and louder ecstasies of whining, and we would stand round cheering him on until his teeth reinforced his front paws in the work of excavation. We were convinced that one day he would dig deep enough for his scufflings to bring up a crock of gold, a bag of rubies or moidores or a casket of pieces-of-eight – but he never did. And the irony of it was that some years after we had grown up and gone away, a contractor obtained permission to level the Field for gravel and sand, and in the process unearthed a big hoard of Roman pottery containing fragments unusual and well-preserved enough to find a home in the British Museum.

The oak-tree I have referred to had great height and girth: it was even said that Windsor Forest had once spread thus far, and indeed the last enchantments of Herne the Hunter seemed to linger among its huge, antlered branches. These sprang out from the trunk too high up to make the tree climbable, but around its base and between its exposed roots were holes big enough for a child to poke his head into, and imagination would furnish the dark interior with alluring stairways and corridors. The crevices in the bark were hiding places for clues in treasure-hunts; yellow underwing moths would dash out from the piles of dead leaves among the roots, swerving this way and that in drunken zig-zags when they reached the sunlight beyond, and buff-tip moth caterpillars in their yellow and black livery and with their black helmeted heads would in due season descend in troops to find a suitable place in the ground for turning into chrysalids. When the grass had been cut and the hay spread in swathes, fragrant and silvery, the great mottled circle of shade and sunbeam around the trunk made a delightful spot for a picnic – whether real with buns and bread-and-butter and paste and tea from a metal pot – or pretence for dolls and teddy-bears, with acorns and oak-apples as substitute cakes and biscuits served on miniature enamel plates. The acorn-cups that lay about everywhere might well have been discarded after use at a midnight festival by more diaphanous beings. If I were more than usually lazy I would lie on my back, musing and dreaming, and look up between half-closed eyelids at the entwined branches and myriad leaves, until the delicious reverie became deep enough to bring a sense of being drawn upward through layer after layer of shade and shine, up and up into the infinite blue above – when there would come a jolt as someone called, 'Wake up! Tea's been here for ages, and there's only one bun left.'

In writing of our oak, I am reminded of an incident my brother used to tell me of, which occurred many years later when he was on leave during the last war from his anti-aircraft battery in the East End of London. One summer afternoon during a walk through an unfamiliar labyrinth of Somerset lanes, he came to a tiny village, and here, in front of the church, was a triangle of grass, in the centre of which stood a big oak. It was evidently an ancient tree, for great bare branches stood out like the spokes of a broken wheel above scanty tufts of greenery, yet enough leaves remained to offer shade in the hot sunshine, and he decided that it would be a pleasant spot for a rest. So he lay down on his back; and as he looked up through the overarching boughs, the rustle of the leaves and the interplay of light among them took him at once in spirit to far off afternoons beneath the family oak-tree in the Field, when scarcely a rumour of the catastrophe that had then befallen the world disturbed the security of childhood – a security deeper than he could feel now, even in this respite from the din of gunfire and exploding bomb. He had gone on to speculate, he used to say, on the numbers of men and women, old and young, dead and gone, who in every mood must have resorted to the shade of the tree. Through how many previous wars, he asked himself, had it stood there, through how many other 'battles long ago' – giving refuge, it might be, to a straggler in desperate flight from Sedgemoor when the young tree had already gained maturity. Musing on such things he had fallen asleep – to be woken with a start and a feeling of unease. Two men were standing over him, one with an axe, the other with a chain-saw.

'Excuse me, Sir,' said one, 'for disturbing your rest, but the old tree's time is up. We have orders from the Council to cut 'un down as being a danger to the public. A pity 'e couldn't bide a bit longer, seeing as how 'e's stood there so long. But there 'tez.'

My brother could think of nothing to say: bewilderment and sadness together overcame him. He walked away as quickly as he could, dreading to hear the first stroke of the axe; but presently, when he had gone a little distance, the whine of the saw just reached him. The sound, he told me, used to come back to him later at the gunsite when, amid fiercer preoccupations, it gave him pause to wonder at the strange hap that had made him the last human being of a long succession to find rest and shelter beneath that tree.

I cannot refrain in this context from quoting part of Thomas Campbell's poem 'The Beech Tree's Petition', hoping that his endangered tree in 1800 was spared the fate of my brother's oak in 1943:

Thrice twenty summers I have seen
The sky grow bright, the forest green;
And many a wintry wind have stood
In bloomless, fruitless solitude.
Since childhood, in my rustling bower
First spent its sweet and sportive hour;
Since youthful lovers in my shade
Their vows of truth and rapture made -
And on my trunk's surviving frame
Carv'd many a long-forgotten name.
Oh! by the sighs of gentle sound
First breathed upon this sacred ground -
By all that love hath whisper'd here,
Or beauty heard with ravish'd ear.
As love's own altar honour me -
Spare, woodman, spare the Beechen Tree.

BLUES

hen we were young the Field swarmed with small butterflies: azure blues, like bright chippings from the sky, small heaths which lay on their grey and sandy-brown sides and cast up reproachful looks from the black mimic eyes on their forewings, meadow browns flopping and sidling and lolloping through the grass stems, and busy brisk little coppers that hardly paused to show off their brightly burnished wings. The coppers were often to be seen in the garden, outshining even the marigolds that my mother loved; but somehow I associate them with our Field playground, where sheep's sorrel, almost as fiery red as the coppers' wings, and ox-eye daisies and deep blue sheepsbit flourished in the sandy soil. With what joy have I met and met again through life with these beautiful little creatures, my mind running back to the Field it may be, or to some cliff-top or patch of downland where harebells blow and the air is sharp with the tang of thyme! In recent years, alas, the numbers of these field-loving butterflies have grown less and less, until now, whenever I am fortunate enough to see one, I am constrained to utter a prayer of thankfulness that it has survived and a word of congratulation on its having done so!

Mention of the blues – so distinct in their very essence from Negro song or fits of melancholy – reminds me of expeditions to the North Downs in search of two of the less common varieties, the adonis and the chalk-hill, which did not inhabit our familiar fields. The beautiful little holly blue was only an occasional visitor, usually to a particular clump of glittering ivy; my most vivid mind-picture of its kind happens to be of a little flock wandering among tamarisk bushes along the shore at Abbotsbury on the Dorset coast, when their creamy blue wings speckled on their undersides with black, the green of the feathery, fronded leaves and the rosy-tasseled flowers formed a blending of colours so lovely that no wonder I still delight in its memory.

Our expeditions to the Downs took place on Saturday afternoons, in one of the station taxis, for my father could not drive and did not then run a car of his own. We travelled in a Unic landaulette with a very low bonnet, its exterior bodywork caparisoned in brass and its interior puffy and padded with heavy grey cording. On either side of the back seat hung a handle, like a short corpulent dressing-gown cord, by which the occupants could pull themselves up; and there were little folding seats embedded in the partition between the back and the driver's compartment that pulled out to rest on stiff steel legs among the shaggy hairs of the mat. An unforgettable soggy smell disappeared when the hood was opened and folded back – which it always was on those occasions – but it was especially pervasive when, on winter evenings, the vehicle conveyed us, spruced up and unwilling, to local parties. Our journeys to the Downs seldom went without a hitch, punctures were not infrequent, causing maddening delays, and once, halfway up the hill to Newlands Corner, we stuck, had to run back, turn round at the bottom and achieve the ascent in reverse. Occasionally we went by train. We would bicycle to the station, take a local train to Guildford, where we would wait in impatience for our father's train from town, and then we would all board another local train that pottered puffing through Shalford, Chilworth, Albury, Gomshall and so on until it deposited us at our goal, Betchworth, since it was the Downs to the north of that village that bred the greatest number of the blues we were seeking.

There, on the steep, flower-strewn slopes, beside the white, deep rutted paths, or in the shelter of small quarries overhung with old-man's-beard, fruiting brambles and berried wayfaring trees, danced male adonises and chalk-hills in dozens. In contrasted shades of blue, the wings of the one were to the wings of the other as zircons are to aquamarines, the one flashing like an electric spark, the other with a softer, milkier gleam; and less conspicuous among them jigged their sober-coloured consorts. Though we took less heed of them, no less brilliant and even more diverse in colour were the flowers; harebell and rampion and field gentian; centaury and thyme and squinancy wort; mousear hawkweed and yellow wort; eyebright and fairy flax; and clustered bell-flower – a farrago of colours, dark blue and light blue, coral and rose, yellow and gold, purest white and deepest purple. A bunch of them – such as we sometimes took home for my mother, though it was somewhat tired, like ourselves, by the time they reached her – was as bright as a casket of jewels, yet more to be prized, for it had a bonus of delicious smells.

The rarest and noblest of all the blues, *Arion*, we were also lucky enough to meet with; not indeed in Surrey, nor yet in its recognised haunts in Gloucestershire and Cornwall. This splendid butterfly (whose portrait has even graced an issue of postage stamps) is now said to be extinct in this country (1987), and entomologists will hardly believe my statement that in the 'twenties we found quite a number in North Devon, admittedly not far

from the Cornish border. There was something about their flight and the violet blue of their ink-blotched, black-bordered wings which, irrespective of size, singled them out from others among the heather and thyme on a cliff-top, or in one sheltered combe, through which a stream twisted in slides and sallies towards the cliff-edge where it fell in a silver mane almost onto the shore. One afternoon, higher up that valley, we observed (with disapproval) another hunter with a net – a thin, rather gaunt figure peering into a gorse bush. My father, in his usual polite way, went up to him, my brother and I hanging back. In conversation the stranger revealed that he was an authority on beetles and had lately been over to Lundy, where he had found 'beetle after beetle new to Britain' – an observation that has passed into the family language. But here, in North Devon, he added in tones of disgust, there was little of interest. This goaded my brother into speech.

'Aren't large blues of interest?' he demanded.

'What do you mean?' was the reply. 'You haven't found large blues round here I'll be bound.'

'Haven't we, though?' exclaimed my brother. 'Come with us and we'll show you.'

Down the combe we led him to a sunny, sheltered basin where the stream made a wide curve. *Arion* 'played up' splendidly and the coleopterist was confounded. The large blue, as every entomologist knows, has a most curious life history, requiring – to cut a long story short – the assistance of ants to complete the maturity of its caterpillar. At once our acquaintance fell on his knees to examine an ants' nest, for it transpired that our noble Arions had little appeal for him; he was intent only on finding an uncommon beetle whose habit is to consort with the caterpillars that feed on the grubs of the ants that live in the ant-hills. To this day I think of it as another version of 'The House that Jack Built'.

FIELD SONGSTERS

It hardly needs saying that the Field was a spring-board for skylarks. The first cheerful notes of the invisible climber as they dropped across the garden on a dark February morning were greeted with almost as much excitement as the blackbird's tentative warble or the drumming of the snipe: to my ear they give no hint of reflectiveness or melancholy, but are a wellspring of promise and hope. But is there anything fresh to say about a skylark's song? The poets have said it all before. I once beguiled some lonely hours in a wartime billet by making my own anthology of poems about birds, or lines describing them – I had only limited access to a library, so my task was a constant bafflement, lines at the back of my memory denying me their source – and I noticed that except for the nightingale the skylark gained the greatest number of entries. It was hard to decide which lines I liked best. Shakespeare, as always, springs to the heart of the matter: the 'tirra-lirra' of Autolycus exactly describes the slightly jerky, upward-stepping movement of the song, and what lovelier image is there than that of the singer at Heaven's gate? Other poets have sought to crystalise their experience in a phrase: Tennyson's 'sightless song', for instance, or Coleridge with his 'Angel in the clouds'. Shelley's Ode, though making for the bird too large assumptions, is magnificent poetry none the less, and the lilt of the short lines in each verse followed by the long alexandrine, does reflect the measure of the song. Moreover, Hardy has contrived to enhance for later readers the beauty of the poem by musing on the whereabouts of the 'tiny pinch of priceless dust' which is all that remains of the bird that inspired the bard 'to win Ecstatic heights in thought and rhyme'. And there is Meredith's *tour de force*, 'The Lark Ascending', reinforced by extraneous aid, the music of Vaughan Williams.

He rises and begins to round,
He drops the silver chain of sound,

85

> *Of many links without a break,*
> *In chirrup, whistle, slur and shake.*
> *All intervolved and spreading wide,*
> *Like water-dimples down a tide*
> *Where ripple ripple overcurls*
> *And eddy into eddy whirls . . .*

Both the variety and regularity of the song are caught here and our own gaze can follow the poet's in the wake of the upward flight of the bird. Yet for me the sheer virtuosity of the poem, with its verbal jugglery and crowded metaphor confuses and distorts; it does not strike home to my heart – my human heart, after all – as does the second and more sober of Wordsworth's eulogies. The etherial *minstrel*, the *pilgrim* of the skies: those two words alone spring the imagination, their overtones propelling its wings. Where will you find in all English poetry a lovelier line than 'A privacy of glorious light is thine'? And the final couplet, without attributing to the bird human sentiments or emotions makes the deeply affecting comment of a noble mind:

> *Type of the wise who soar, but never roam –*
> *True to the kindred points of Heaven and Home.*

Writing of skylarks and the response of human beings to their charm, I cannot forebear to refer to St Francis of Assisi, who had a particular affection for them, and it does not seem to me to matter in the least whether the birds he loved were crested larks or not – though I admit I have seen crested larks on the open ground that drops down from the saint's hill-top city and surrounds the Portiuncola. My affection for both bird and saint may justify a long quotation from *The Mirror of Perfection*:

Blessed Francis, wholly wrapped up in the love of God, discerned perfectly the goodness of God not only in his own soul, now adorned with the perfection of virtue, but in every creature. On account of which he had a singular and intimate love of creatures, especially those in which was figured anything pertaining to God or the Order. Whence above all other birds he loved a certain little bird which is called the lark, or by the people, the cowled lark. And he used to say of it, 'Sister Lark hath a cowl like a Religious; and she is a humble bird, because she goes willingly by the road to find there any food. And if she comes upon it in foulness, she draws it and eats it. But flying she praises God very sweetly like a good Religious, despising earthly things, whose conversation is always in the heavens, and whose intent is always to the praise of God. Her clothes are like to the earth (that is her feathers) and she gives an example to Religious that they should not have delicate and coloured garments, but vile in price and colour, as earth is viler than the other elements.' And because he perceived this in them, he looked on them most willingly. Therefore it pleased the Lord, that these most holy little birds should show some signs of affection towards him in the hour of his death. For late on the Saturday, after vespers, before the night in which he passed away to the Lord, a great multitude of that kind of birds called larks came on the roof of the house where he was lying; and flying about, made a wheel like a circle round the roof, and sweetly singing, seemed likewise to praise the Lord. '

In Summer, a cheerful cousin of the skylark had a favourite perch on one of the trees that lent over the fence from the garden into the Field. The tree-pipit is a bird that has two songs, one rich and melodious sung usually in concealment among the topmost branches of a bush or tree, and the other a cascade of quick, slithering notes which, when the bird has made a leap twenty feet or so into the air, accompany its slow dive earthward, wings raised and tail spread; yet it never, or not in my experience, actually reaches the ground, but towards the bottom of a dive makes a sudden level swerve to alight on some convenient perch. The song, the soar and the dive are indulged in again and again. The joy of the little parachutist is as plain as the performance is deliberate in showing off his expert control – perhaps to his mate hidden in her nest in the long grass – and gives recurring delight to the human watcher. Search the Field as we might for the nest, we never found it, and it was not until years later that I became cleverer, or luckier. The most beautifully placed nest I have ever seen was on the side of a deeply cleft valley between beech woods in the Chilterns, where the nest containing four or five eggs sprinkled all over with rich, chocolate-coloured markings lay beneath a tussock surrounded by an arabesque of butterfly orchids, the white-winged shapes of the flowers like a group of dancers in 'Les Sylphides' as viewed from 'the Gods'.

THE POND

y favourite spot in the garden – after my oak-tree in the Wild Patch – was the far south-east corner, where it jutted out in the shape of an arrow-head into the water-meadows. The Ditch (as we called it) ran alongside and emptied such water as it could boast into the Bourne a few yards further on: the Bourne itself was hardly eight feet wide. At the very tip of the arrow stood another big oak-tree, a little smaller than the one in the Field, but like it in having a hole that could almost be crawled into and many enticing crevices between the roots. The interior of the hole stretched upwards into a darkness that the eye, unlike the imagination, could not penetrate and its walls had been worn by time and decay into a series of grooves and fissures like stairways leading to I knew not what faery kingdoms: Lyonesse, Eldorado, Lilliput, Cathay. Hardly less enticing, I remember, was a tendril of ivy growing straight up the trunk, each leaf attached to the main stem at as regular intervals as the rungs of a ladder. If there had been handy a piece of one of Alice's mushrooms, a nibble or two would have made me small enough to climb up, as Jack did his beanstalk, to some turreted castle among the clouds.

It was in this peaceful, yet agreeably haunted, spot that one Summer evening I experienced a few moments of terror. I was perhaps ankle-deep in a reverie that had taken me some distance into one of those fancied king-doms, when I became aware of an indeterminate white shape floating this way and that along the Bourne as it wound its way across the meadow. In the slanting sunlight it made me think of a white handkerchief waved by someone in need of help. As the shape glided nearer I realised that it was merely a hunting barn owl, and with a sense of relief I watched in admira-tion its perfect control of wings that made no sound. All of a sudden the owl turned in my direction and began to fly straight at my oak-tree. Relief turned to alarm as on and on it came, the eyes fixed and prominent in the hooded face. Nearer and nearer loomed those black eyes, boring, boring into the very heart of me. In my terror I had become a small rodent at the point of death. That was the moment for the bird itself to sense hostility, for it swung away in a swerve so violent that I could now hear the pinions quiver. I had shut my eyes and when I opened them a few moments later the menace had dwindled once more into a pennant silently flapping above the reeds.

Behind the oak lay a small pond – the Pond, as we always called it. Round it grew one or two alders and sallows and clumps of the royal fern *Osmunda*, of which the original plant my father had brought at some remote period from the banks of the River Dart. In Summer the water put on a cloak of green weed so closely woven that it looked like the baize on our bagatelle board, and as the season advanced a great dragon-fly, helmeted in the fashion of a being from outer space, swooped and swung across it with clashing wings, a hunter as fierce as any hawk or leopard. Once, but only once, as I remember, there came a shrill cry, a spark of blue, a burning glow, then silence; a kingfisher had come and gone.

The shallow edges of the Pond were fruitful nurseries for tadpoles when they had emerged from the skeins of spawn (reminding one horribly of the tapioca that was served up for pudding on occasional black days and could only be swallowed if smothered in raspberry jam). The wriggling forms of the tadpoles were an entertainment in themselves, especially when on sunny days they were repeated by their shadows on the mud beneath. In places where the water had not yet put on its cloak of weed the topsy-turvy water-boatmen, like inverted sea-planes, pursued their piratical forays, also repeated by their shadows, and teams of whirligig beetles spun round and round on the surface, glittering like the stars from the sparklers we were allowed to hold in our hands at Christmas time. Even more delightful than the tadpoles were the yellow and black frogs they turned into, now tail-less and be-legged, which rustled and jumped through the Wild Patch close by and seemed never to be on other than good terms with those other vaulters, the grasshoppers. We much enjoyed chasing and picking up the frogs, but the reproachful look in their globular black and yellow eyes and the fear that the pulse-beats in their throats might suddenly stop soon persuaded us to put them back from hot hand to cool grass.

On the far side of the Pond was the plank fence I have mentioned dividing the garden from the Field; the trunks and branches cast a filigree of shadows upon its greenish boards. One day a small blob began to move up one side of a tree's shadow and for a moment I thought I had imagined it; but presently it appeared on the other side a little further up, with a curved projection which could only indicate a beak. Turning to look at the tree itself I saw a small mouse-like creature clinging to the trunk, its back beautifully speckled with brown and cream and with a breast so white that it caught the light with the body's every turn and twist.

The tree-creeper, for such it was, must surely be held in special affection by every bird-lover. If it is not uncommon, it is rare enough for any encounter with it to put him in a good humour! Yet in saying that, I think I do the bird an injustice, for it is its charming ways – the flickering movements, the spirals of its climb, the darts and sallies and vibrant probings into the crevices of the bark – that bring a delight in themselves quite unconnected with rarity. The bird, too, will break suddenly into song, not strong or melodious, but endearing, like itself, no more than a trill which seems to claim, 'see, see, see, see, prrretty me!' Its first choice of site for its nest – it has various choices – may fairly be said to be unique: the cavity formed when a piece of bark has leant away from the trunk of a tree to provide in between a shelter deep and snug. Except for the long-tailed tit, no bird, I fancy, stuffs its nest with so many feathers. It may well be far-fetched to suggest that this partiality endears the two species to each other, but I have often noticed that in winter a flock of long-tailed tits has its attendant creeper.

I remember watching with my brother when we were both young a creeper building its nest in a tall tree by the canal near Pipers Hill. We stood for some time waiting for the bird to return in see-sawing flight to the base of the tree and wondering which way it would wind upward until it reached the chosen crevice. It was one of those slight experiences which some caprice of memory lodges in the mind, on this occasion the mind of each of us; for many years later, long after we had grown up and left home, on a Sunday morning outing from London in spring-time, we both recalled the building creeper as we came near the old nesting-site and wondered whether we might find that some descendant had followed its ancestor's example and decided to make its nest there. For a few moments we could not identify the tree, and as it was time to eat our sandwiches we sat down on a log overgrown with lengthening grass. We had hardly taken a bite before it struck us that our seat was the creeper's tree. We both at once recalled Cowper's poem about the felled poplars which our old Headmaster had loved and made us learn by heart:

> *Twelve years have elapsed since I first took a view*
> *Of my favourite field, and the bank where they grew;*
> *And now in the grass behold they are laid,*
> *And the tree is my seat that once lent me a shade . . .*

> *'Tis a sight to engage me, if anything can,*
> *To muse on the perishing pleasures of man;*

91

Though his life be a dream, his enjoyments, I see,
Have a being less durable even than he.

THE WATER-MEADOWS

he Water-meadows and the Bourne belonged to each other: it is hard to think of them individually, each partaking of the other's essence. I used sometimes to wonder whether the Bourne stuck always to its meandering course, for one day a loop seemed to go in one direction and the next in another, and the flowers and reeds along its borders to change with it. And oh! how lovely were the flowers that grew there in Summer: tossing plumes of meadowsweet and spires of loose-strife, purple and yellow willow-herb (the former so delightfully nicknamed codlins and cream) and, loveliest of all, the irises with their golden wings. Then, as I grew older, I noticed less noticeable flowers like bur marigold, and gipsywort and skull-cap. Out of the water itself sprang clumps of lilac-pale water plantain and on its surface lay the green triangles of arrow-heads with their white flowers centred with imperial purple.

The Bourne was the dwelling-place of many water-voles. We were correct in not liking to call them 'rats', even though the most celebrated scion of their clan was called 'Ratty', who naturally held a treasured place in our affections. It was possible to creep along the bank on the garden side – since the stream was too wide to jump across and too deep and muddy to wade – in the shelter of the palisade of reeds and flags and wait for one to come swimming past almost beneath our feet; but the little swimmer was always too sharp-eyed for us and we would hear a plop as he dived and see only the file of bubbles that marked his progress towards the far side. There a nose would rise above the surface and the top half of a brown, furry body go gliding along beneath the shelter of the bank, the legs paddling vigorously like a swimming dog's. We discovered that as well as holes in the side of the bank there would be communicating burrows leading up in the manner of escape-hatches to the flat ground above, where at intervals there were small patches of close-cropped grass and other herbage. The capers the voles cut on these little lawns – and imagination could play with all kinds of games

93

and dances, or even picnic parties – we were never lucky enough to witness. We noticed also that they had set aside certain places for doing what my father called 'Number Two', but which I should now, I suppose, call latrines.

The closest encounter I had with a water-vole came unexpectedly. The skiff we used for boating expeditions on the canal beyond the water-meadows was moored one afternoon close to the bank and I was lying in the stern engrossed in a book. I had been eating an apple and had dropped the core into the water on the bank side. An alien susurrus, if that is the word – quite unconnected with the tapping of Blind Pew's stick, the clash of assegais, the surge of waves on a coral island, or whatever other sound my book was persuading me to attend to at that moment – began to impinge on my consciousness and it dawned on me that it belonged to the present Summer afternoon in my own homeland. Slowly turning my head in the direction of the sound, I saw not two feet away 'Ratty' himself sitting on his haunches on a little beach of sand, my apple-core between his fore paws, quietly munching; the twinkle in his eyes and the wriggle of his whiskers showed how much he was enjoying the unfamiliar delicacy. We looked at each other for a long time (was it in shared amusement?), as he turned the core over and over with his deft fingers and bit into it with his little narrow teeth. When there was nothing left, a mere flick of his body sent him back into his hole and I saw him no more. I do not think that in the whole of my life I have been closer than I was then to a wild animal in its own haunts.

The water-meadows themselves stretched to the right of the garden as far as the Canal, and on the left to the windings of the River Wey; but ahead to Infinity. It was a little infinity, if the expression can be allowed, for at the back of the flower-strewn levels and small boggy plantations where kingcups glowed there were gathered countless trees growing fainter in shape and colour towards a long, gently undulating line of hills – hills that might, for all we knew, have been the 'Delectable Mountains' looking yet further to an unimaginable 'beyond' where gleamed the Celestial City and all its towers. (That the 'city' may in fact have been Guildford or Dorking was no concern of ours.)

In the early Summer, before haymaking, ragged robin and lady's smock, sorrel and buttercups and oxeye daisies and all the silvery and pinkish grass-plumes gave with their myriad dots and dabs of colour the effect of a painting by a *pointilliste* master. Yet as I look back I think the meadows were at their most beautiful in early Spring when flood-water spread now here, now there, wayward sheets of blue and silver, when the rushes ran molten gold across the levels of young green and the still leafless willows stood burning with the glow of a forge fire.

It was then that the snipe began their mystic drumming and the lapwing to toss their black and white shapes into the air, uttering their soaring, then swooping cries of *pee-oo-wit, wit, wit*: the uprush of the wings and the tumbling falls seemed to imitate the cries, matching sight with sound. Those beautiful movements, I used to think, were like fountains as they shoot up, curve over and let fall their scattered drops. And often as they wheeled and swooped the air would reverberate with the measured beating of their wings. Each year another kind of bird would come to join the snipe and lapwing in a distinctive trio. These were the redshank, and like the other two their slim forms turned promptly to silver when the sunlight caught them. Their piping, too, had silvery tones which sent a light carillon across the meadows, as though someone were shaking a hand-bell. If a bird were alarmed the notes would scramble from its scarlet beak in a prolonged trill as it sprang from the rushes and came to a stand on legs no less scarlet on some favoured post. Another high-pitched call would mingle with the trills of the redshank, for the snipe, when not riding their aerial switchback or whizzing earthward in headlong plunges, would burst into excited cries of *chippi, chippi, chippi, chip, chip, chip* as they made a landfall among the rushes, or received some provocation to swoop up to the top of a fence and express their feelings there.

How clearly the characteristic calls of these three – snipe, lapwing, redshank – so dissimilar, yet blending with the harmony of instruments in a string trio, sound in my mind as I sit here writing more than half a century since I last heard them together! I think of them as a benediction. I remember that on the morning of the very day we left Pipers Hill for ever they were the sounds that rang in my ears. Their actual tones may have been silenced by human encroachment as the years passed, but in memory, like 'music when soft voices die', they still vibrate.

MALLARD

he only species of wild duck that I can recall visiting the water-meadows is the mallard. Everyone, even the most inveterate town-dweller, knows this charming duck, since no municipal pond or lake is surely without a small flock: the dandy drakes, with their glossy green heads, purple 'beauty spots' on their wings and a jaunty curlycue on their tails, swimming a little ahead of their soberly dressed consorts, who look so comfortable and motherly and wear an expression of such contented amiability. Yet, when in flight, they shed altogether this cosy, domestic air and achieve an effect of wildness and untamed freedom, their long necks and widespread, pointed wings giving them the appearance of arrows shot from a great distance across the sky. A pair flying over the garden at home usually provoked a cry of 'Quick, look!' and made us pause in whatever we might be doing to follow their swift progress as they tilted and turned and planed, head and necks thrust forward and legs straight down in search of some smooth stretch of the Bourne out of view between the reeds. At night in springtime, when the moon lit up the garden – and especially when the floods were out – they were undoubtedly at carnival in celebration of their weddings, for again and again their chuckles would break across the stillness and the sky tingle with the whinnying of their wings.

The recollection of our mallard – if I may use the possessive – sends my mind forward from childhood to the most memorable of all my encounters with a bird that is at home as much in towns as on a desolate salting. Indeed it was an encounter as strange as any I have had with a wild creature, when time itself – to borrow a phrase of Hardy's – 'closed up like a fan'. To convey its haunting quality requires some space for sketching in the background.

My brother and I had the good fortune to be invited to Ireland regularly in the years before the last War by an elderly couple whose only child, a son, my brother's particular crony at school, had been killed in a riding accident.

Our hostess had her own ideas about time. I do not mean that she was unpunctual, or regarded unpunctuality with indifference; on the contrary, she was never known to be late for a meal or an appointment and did not expect to be kept waiting herself. It was on the metaphysical plane that she gave rein to her theories. They were based (in so far as I could follow her exposition) on a rejection of the concepts of past, present and future, which she held to be arbitrary divisions of the indivisble invented for the convenience of unperceptive minds. 'There is no such thing as Time,' she would affirm in a tone and with an emphasis positively sibylline; and she would pronounce the words with a rap of her ebony cigarette holder on the rosewood table at her elbow and with her head turned so that the small, deep-set brown eyes might gaze out through the window, up the garden and away to the blue rim of the Wicklow mountains bridging the gaps between the lime-trees.

She would expound her views to me in the drawing-room on a Summer evening, when the small Rockingham coffee-cups had been taken away by the white-capped, stiff-cuffed parlourmaid from Kerry and my brother and our host had repaired to the study to play duets: transcriptions of Mendelssohn's overture to *Ruy Blas* or Handel's *Water Music*, or a selection from *The Marriage of Figaro*. Their performance, muted by closed doors, would evoke another of her *pronunciamenti*, uttered this time with a mischievous lilt of the voice and gleam of the eye: 'I can't bear duets – either to play them or to listen to them;' and it was clear that no plea of custom or marital indulgence, nor yet the passage of the conventional sort of time, would ever reconcile them to her taste.

For all that, the notes still sound in memory; and there has lingered also down the years a harmony of scents peculiar to the room: an amalgam of the polish on the furniture, the *pot-pourri* in the Ch'ien Lung bowl, the jasmine and Betty Uprichard roses nodding at the open windows, the faded pages and leather bindings of the old books – volumes of Swift and Gray and Maria Edgeworth – that kept straying from their shelves to the table beside her chair, and the smoke of the single Turkish cigarette that she allowed herself each evening.

For this last she would perform without fail a little ritual. She prided herself on the fine texture and gleaming whiteness of her hair – it was her only vanity – and having heard with alarm that nicotine might stain it yellow, she made sure that her head should be well covered while she smoked. She kept for that purpose, in a drawer of her bureau, a strip of flowered brocade, which she would carefully wind round her head. Thus coifed, she would return to her tall chair, light up with relish, and leaning back, while the blue smoke rose in a harmless spiral about the improvised turban, remark with a smile: 'One day you will find I have taken to a hookah.' Then on she would go about time.

As I listened, my attention was apt to wander. I would look at the pictures on the dark green walls – a formal Victorian portrait, an oil by Yeats, with its plangent blues and greens and crimsons, a small Turner water-colour on an easel, depicting a sunlit Italian city perched on a hill; or through the window to the garden where the panoply of roses gleamed and a flycatcher sallied from some hidden observation post with tireless dart and hover. There was in truth a timeless – or at least a time-defying – quality about that room.

The past was ever present for my hostess, another topic of inexhaustible charm being her experiences of Dublin society in the 'nineties as a girl newly arrived from England; the balls, the garden parties, the soirées, the excursions by carriage, the stylish days at the races. Yet at the heart of that gay blooming lurked the canker of a profound shyness and I fancied that if it had not been for the affectionate solicitude of a woman much older than herself, she would have fallen out of the social steeplechase far sooner than she did.

A small photograph of her friend Moira stood in a silver frame on the bureau. It showed a face at once serious and playful, with large wide-set eyes just tilted upwards at the corners beneath dark eyebrows, a broad forehead, and two fine wings of grey hair flung back from a centre parting. My hostess would turn to the photograph now and then, as though to consult her friend's opinion, only to turn away again with a little sigh or chuckle at the stubborn inaccessibility of the dead.

One day, as we were returning from a morning's shopping in the city, she was unusually pensive. At luncheon, she observed sharply with no apparent relevance: 'How foolish it is to be upset when the inevitable happens, but it's a folly I fall into often enough!' We waited for her to explain. 'You know, of course, that dear Moira's house has been empty for a long time. I always knew that it was too big and rambling to be lived in again, but the place has been a symbol for me all these years and I had hoped vainly enough that the garden and the park and the exquisite lake' – she was silent for a moment – 'might somehow be preserved. But I heard today that the whole property was sold some months ago for development as a housing estate and that work has already begun. After Moira's death I could never bring myself to go there but now I feel I must venture once more, while the place is still recognisable. Would you like to come?'

The following afternoon we drove to the far side of the city, and in response to the directions she gave through the corded speaking tube, the chauffeur brought us at length along a road bordered on one side by a high wall, which had been hacked through in more than one place to admit builders' lorries. 'The entrance is just along on the left,' my friend called, and we came soon to a dilapidated lodge beside tall iron gates in an embrasure. The chauffeur could get no reply from the lodge and the gates were bound together inexorably by a chain.

My friend was not to be baffled, and getting out of the car she advanced to a wicket at the side half hidden by an overgrown shrub and gave it a sharp push. It yielded with a little dismal groan. She was not much of a walker, but she set off up the drive with surprising resilience, quite undisconcerted by the ruts and potholes and averting her eyes from the park, which was already branded with new roadways and heaped with sand, bricks, planks and lengths of piping, and where the trunks of felled trees, some chained together, lay about like slaughtered galley slaves. A strange silence weighed upon everything. It was the workmen's half-day and there was no sound or movement anywhere. The mechanism of development had for a while ceased even to tick.

The drive led on through a tunnel of laurel and yew into what had been a circular sweep of gravel in front of the house. The tall Georgian building was still erect, but sightless and cadaverous, as if its jaw had dropped. My friend gave a slight shudder and turned away. 'It is dead,' she murmured. 'Let us try the lake. That never altered – could not alter. Moira loved it. She declared its beauty was imperishable. Hardly a day went by but she walked across to it, and whatever her mood, she felt it respond with the understanding of a friend. If anything in particular troubled or pleased her, she would say: "I will tell the wild duck about it."' We had come through a swing gate in the iron palings and struck off across a stretch of the park as yet untouched by the builders, and were walking with a little difficulty through grass that through lack of care had grown into wiry tussocks.

She stopped abruptly. 'I saw the wild duck many times. Whenever Moira came to the water's edge they would appear from nowhere, conjured as if by magic from the sky. They would wheel downward on their singing wings, as she described them, and greet her in their quiet voices. How indignant she was if anyone dared to speak of her wild duck as quacking!'

We went on again at a slow pace among the brown and blue butterflies glancing over the flowers of yellow bedstraw, the fume of which was the most positive element in the hush of the afternoon. Even the sun, though its presence was everywhere, seemed to have dozed off behind a curtain of haze. We were nearing the lake now, but could not yet see it for the silver-headed willows and dark alders and the palisade of reeds that grew along the margin. Huge somnolent elms were gathered round, and beyond them stretched the mountains. A new scent was beginning to fill the air – a scent that for me is redolent of the bindings and pages of old books. It streamed

from the drifts of meadowsweet at the landward edge of the reeds, their cloudy plumes thronging the banks.

We must have followed the course of a hidden path for we had come to a gap in the reeds and the remnants of a landing-stage. The water lay before us. It was quite still and there was enough of it yet among the encroaching reeds to mirror everything around in flawless colour and outline. We stopped and the silence gathered closer.

It was with a perceptible effort that my friend began to speak: 'This was the very spot where Moira would come and talk to the wild duck. I remember it distinctly now. She would stand in line with the reflection of that big tree where its head reaches down to touch the tip of the landing-stage. How quiet it is, and how unchanged!'

She had hardly finished, when my ear caught a sound groping through the enveloping stillness – a sound that told me her revisitation had been perceived. She noticed it too and glanced upward. 'Look!' she whispered. A flock of mallard in a neat wedge had appeared from nowhere – conjured, as she had said, out of the sky – and came slanting down towards the lake. When the birds were some twenty feet above the water they flew level and in line, their bright plumage making a ribbon of varied colour against the sombre green of the trees.

Just opposite the gap they dipped, and, putting out their feet, sped forward and downward one after the other into the water, throwing up light flurries of spray. One shook its head, another its tail, another a foot; then all composed themselves, locked their wings, turned and swam quietly past us as though in salute. They turned and passed again. A moment more and they were in flight; and as we stood there among the meadowsweet, we could hear no sound at all but the gradually diminishing music of their wings.

MOSS-CUPS AND SPURGE LAUREL

ne morning, very early in the year, as we walked along a deep-hedged lane a mile or so from home, my father stopped suddenly and pointed with that questing walking-stick of his to something in the bank that gleamed bright red – as bright almost, so it seemed in its dark surroundings, as the rear reflector on my new bicycle! When we looked more closely we saw that it was a tiny cup-shaped 'toadstool' clinging to a mossy stump. I remember putting out my finger to touch it and drawing back with a slight recoil at the contrast between the glow of its complexion and the chill fleshiness I had touched. It was, though we did not know it at the time, a specimen of the charming miniature fungus known to the mycologist as *Sarcoscypha coccinea* (though its scientific name has a perplexing mutability).

To a child's eye it looked a strange, enchanted thing, made and put there by magic; and even if it was merely a natural evanescent fungus, there is something hardly less enchanting than the persistence in memory of a first encounter with a curious natural object such as this when later years have brought a certain familiarity. As I sit writing on a morning of late January, so distant in place from that Surrey-born moss-cup and so remote in time from its discovery, it strikes me that all such recollections increase in poignancy as we grow older and may be numbered among the very rare compensations of age, with its long memories, which youth, with its short ones, cannot fully enjoy. However this may be, I have come to regard them as cadences in the poetry that Life itself recites.

I must now acknowledge that in this instance my second encounter with a moss-cup has run through my memory in double harness, so to speak, with my first – mainly, I suppose, because it came at an epoch in my life. On the first afternoon of my first day at boarding-school in the West Country, the Headmaster took the new boys for a walk, and as he was a devoted Nature-lover he was at pains to point out to his small charges anything that his keen and practised eye might note: the minute white flowers of whitlow-grass on a wall, the reddening buds on a line of wych-elms, the bottle-green scrolls of uncurling arum leaves. Great was his delight on finding a moss-cup set on a twig in a bed of moss among the hart's-tongue ferns and the new green of hedge-parsley. No less great was his eagerness that we should share his pleasure; and although for two or three years it was natural that he should remain the Headmaster and I one of his pupils, I look back upon the happiness of that walk as sowing the seeds of a friendship that both of us treasured for almost forty years.

Moss-cups are by no means common – at any rate in my experience – so that finding one is always an excitement, as much for the immediate pleasure it affords as for the accompanying associations. A few years ago, my brother and I found one in a Somerset lane which had always looked to be the very place for it, but where I had been unsuccessful in finding it before. We remarked to each other that the re-encounter sent our minds back to what I will call the twin discoveries in the Surrey lane and the Dorset hedgerow which I have been recalling. Our little 'find' was a typical member of its race, in shape round and neat, in colour a warm solid red, like that of a guardsman's tunic, a stick of sealing-wax, a beaker of the newest plastic, a tiddlywink; Leigh Hunt's epithet for holly berries, 'rutilant' is appropriate. The brim of the cup, about half an inch in diameter, was incurved after the fashion of a Victorian moustache-cup, and since it is incontrovertible that every moss-cup is part of a fairy dinner service, it was not unreasonable to suppose that this was the property of an elf with 'handlebars'!

Coccinea is known to 'liberal shepherds' and 'cold maids' by a number of names, none gross that I know of: Jew's ear, Jerusalem star, soldier's cap and scarlet elf cup. Each indicates one or other of its characteristics, the colour having, as I have suggested, a martial ardour, and the curved rim in some specimens a close resemblance to the grooves and twists of an ear – though I know of no connection between the Holy City and the planet Mars, whose ruddy gleam might otherwise provide a likeness, nor have I observed that the Jew has more strikingly voluted ears than the Gentile. It is surprising that no musical similitude has gained currency, since I have found more than one moss-cup that resembles a tiny uplifted trumpet, a likeness reinforced in a shadowy environment by the positive blare of its colour. There is said to be a rare milk-white form, but I have never been lucky enough to find it. May that encounter chance by moonlight!

Around my recent home in Somerset, the New Year always brought me other reminders of that first afternoon walk of my schooldays, for in the hedges and copses thereabout the spurge laurel grows in plenty, and it was a clump of this grave and handsome plant that our Headmaster showed us within a few yards of the spot where the moss-cup was growing. There is nothing but this association to link the two together – except their beauty and that winter breeds them. *Daphne laureola*, to give it its Latin name, is conspicuous enough among the naked undergrowth, yet does not vaunt itself like the cheerful moss-cup. It is cool and darksome and, for all its glossy leaves and upstanding growth, diffident and sad, as though it were in truth the nymph herself bewailing the loss of the nimble legs that carried her out of the reach of the vehement God to a safety now grown somewhat wearisome. The myth derives more probably from *laureola's* brightly-coloured, richly-scented cousin *mezereum*, a plant much less rare in classical Greece than contemporary England and one of more overt attractions. Indeed, Andrew Young, in the second of his two delightful books in which he surveys the wild flowers of this country in prospect and retrospect, supports the somewhat unchivalrous interpretation given to the myth by Marvell (another poet, another Andrew and another plant-lover), who declares:

> *Apollo haunted Daphne so,*
> *Only that She might Laurel grow.*

Laureola may be less brilliant than *mezereum* and less richly scented but its evergreen ruff and cluster of tight-skirted, yellow-green flowers with their hardly perceptible smell lend a quiet distinction to whatever secluded spot it may choose to dwell in.

Not long before his death my brother and I made a sentimental pilgrimage to the very lane where the moss-cup and the spurge laurel (I resume the name by which our Headmaster introduced it) had been growing so close to each other exactly half a century before. The lane itself had hardly altered. We searched in vain for a moss-cup, but we did find a clump of spurge laurel more or less in the same spot we both remembered. We wished our Headmaster could have been with us and half hoped he might be looking on. We both wondered whether it had been there fifty years earlier – perhaps even a hundred, for it is a plant of sturdy growth, well able to stand up to the wear and tear of the seasons. How long, I have often asked myself, have the wild plants that greet me each year in their customary haunts bloomed and faded there? As Walter de la Mare observed in his lovely poem:

> *Very old are the woods;*
> *And the buds that break*
> *Out of the brier's boughs,*
> *When March winds wake,*
> *So old with their beauty are –*
> *Oh, no man knows*

Moss-Cups and Spurge Laurel

*Through what wild centuries
Roves back the rose.*

THE PRIMROSE COPSE

an there be anything fresh to say about a primrose? If so, I doubt my capacity to say it; and yet an experience I had only the other day impels me to venture a few words more.

I cannot claim that primroses – wild primroses – grew in our garden at Pipers Hill, or in any of the hedges that enclosed the neighbouring fields. But about two miles away there was a copse that we used to call the Primrose Copse and it lay on the far side of a field that we called the Cowslip Field; and in it there were some, though not many, tufts of primroses. The copse was always an object of pilgrimage in the Easter holidays and the way to it lay by a footpath bordering the River where we found the caterpillar of the elephant hawk-moth.

The recent experience that I have mentioned was simply this: after a very cold spell of weather in February my wife and I drove down to a lane in south Dorset where we guessed that the first primroses might be showing their pale faces – their sweet, pale faces, if I may be allowed the touch of sentiment. It was sunny and sheltered in the lane and there, to confirm our guess, on a steep bank was a plant bearing a cluster of five or six flowers. I duly bent my head until the soft petals touched my cheek and nose. Once again – oh, thank Heaven, once again! – Providence was allowing me to drink in the smell that of all flower smells is to me the most poignant and the most delicious. The effect upon me was magical. In a moment scene after scene of my life, now lengthened well beyond the psalmist's span, rose before my mind's eye: school-children laughing and exclaiming in the Primrose Copse; a little sister who died in childhood stooping to add to her posy in a Hertfordshire wood while the first cuckoo called; bunches massed together above the panelling of the School Chapel for the Easter Service and round the font at my son's baptism in the Kentish church where my wife and I had been married; rank upon rank along a favoured lane in north Devon, with the gorse bushes at the top of the hedge throwing out their golden largesse against the blue of the sea beyond and the celandines a-glitter along the runnel of water at the bank's foot. Time seemed to close up; the long span of my life contracted to a few visionary moments in which, as it seemed, I perceived the very source of the beauty of our Earth. Old as I was, it was as if I had become eternally young. I could not but whisper to myself a few words of deep thankfulness that once more, yet once more, I had been allowed to look upon those pale faces, each with a little quincunx of deep yellow at its centre, and to inhale the simple incense they offered up to Heaven as their own tribute of praise.

Then, for a few moments, my thoughts dwelt on the joy these fragile flowers had given long before, and would give long after, my own brief span. None of us can guess at the Future, but the Past? Did the unchronicled ancients who built the ramparts high up on the hill over there pause to gaze and to smell? Had the Roman legionaries a chance to break their long marches and rest a brief spell against a primrose bank while they ate their appointed rations? Those conquering Normans, those warring barons, those fugitive Kings and Queens, those plumed Cavaliers and leathern Roundheads, all the pursuers and pursued – had they a moment's leisure, a moment's respite, to consider and reflect, casting, as they hurried on, a glance of envy at some little group of country girls and boys with bunches of primroses clenched in their hands, curiously watching them go by. Yet, as I turned back to look and smell once more, I could not but feel that what matters most is the here and now and the freshness of our response to the present moment's joy. As I walked away there came to me the unspoken prayer that as long as life was granted me I might never suppress or let fail the sort of emotions of thankfulness and praise which then had possession of my heart.

But to return – more than a hundred miles and half a century – to the Primrose Copse. Many sorts of other flowers grew there, all familiar, yet always affectionately greeted each year as they showed their colours again: bluebells, wood anemones (as white and delicate as any I have known), stitchwort, bugle, yellow pimpernel, yellow archangel (or weasel-snout, as dear old 'Johns' goes to the opposite extreme and calls it) and 'lords and ladies', like tiny saints at prayer in jade-green niches. And along the margins of the copse, where they stood on scattered, intricately wrought mats of green, we would greet the flowers of moschatel.

This curious flower is an old favourite of mine. It is not uncommon but hides itself away in shady places like the Primrose Copse, by no means where you hope to find it. The very name that Linnaeus gave it suggests that among its more showy associates it has only a walking-on part, or lurks in the back row of the chorus: *Adoxa moschatellina*, which, being roughly interpreted, means 'little musky one without glory'. It all depends, however, what you mean by glory.

Its height is insignificant – four to five inches at most – and its colour a uniform green, though when you look closely you see that its anthers are bright yellow. These give it an endearing smile – or rather, not one smile, but five, for the flower has that number of faces, four at the side of its head, looking outward, and one on top that gazes straight up at the beholder. You might say that, as in a good portrait, the eyes follow you round. Its local name, the old town clock, has caught an expressive likeness, and since each little coronet of petals is of the order botanists call rotate, there is a suggestion of turning hands and an interior movement. If you put your head down close by a clump of the flowers, no great effort of fancy is needed to see it as a towered city of Lilliput, and when the shadows of the trees flicker across and the wind rocks the tiny crowded belfries, the answering rustle makes a sort of chime. The association with horology becomes closer when there is a chiff chaff about, as there usually was in the Primrose Copse. But you will be lucky if you catch the musk-like scent; I confess to have found it elusive.

It was the Headmaster of my preparatory school who introduced me to moschatel, and to other less familiar flowers: I doubt whether, but for him, we should have noticed the carpets of moschatel in the Primrose Copse. He used to keep an exercise-book in which the first finding of a wild flower each year was noted, and there was brisk competition among flower enthusiasts to see who could obtain the most entries. He had a remarkable knowledge of the local flora, and after tea on Sunday evenings in the Spring and Summer he would come into the Dining-hall and from the various specimens in the hot little bunches we brought for his inspection he could tell us which lanes and field paths we had taken in our afternoon walks. There was something uncanny in his powers of deduction: it was as if his eyes, like the moschatel's, had followed us round.

I remember the occasion when I first found moschatel for myself. It was on a fine Sunday afternoon towards the end of the Easter term and a friend and I were walking in a pleasant valley about a mile from the town. A stream chattered along it, winding through deep banks overhung with hazel and alder and hawthorn. The branches made an enticing tunnel, in which two boys could easily hide themselves while they took off their boots and stockings and paddled.

We hesitated awhile before venturing our feet into the water, not on account of its coldness – though the memory of its icy touch makes me catch my breath – but because we doubted whether such an occupation would be thought proper to a Sunday afternoon and were quite sure that at that time of year it would have been forbidden as likely to give us colds. Nevertheless we determined to dare and were soon up to our knees in water, investigating the network of exposed roots and poking into every hole and crevice in the banks, oblivious alike of the chilly ripples, the pressure of the soles of our feet on the sharp pebbles and the risk of being seen by some officious person who might go back and report us.

It was on rounding a small promontory at the foot of an oak that I found myself looking down on a patch of moschatel. The leaves held out their fresh green palms above the brown earth and five or six little dials were cheerfully smiling. I realised at once that it was early for the flower to be in bloom; that nobody in the school had found it so far that year; and that, as my companion was more interested in 'bugs', as we called them, than flowers, I should not even have to share the honours with him. I picked two or three pieces, stuffed them into the breast pocket of my jacket and continued the exploration. At length we did begin to feel cold, and having dried our feet on our handkerchiefs and put on our stockings and boots, we made our way back to school, as far as we were aware undetected. The sodden handkerchiefs we thrust down a rabbit-hole, since we could think of no way to account for their condition that would satisfy the matron.

I ate my tea in some excitement at the prospect of laying my prize before the Headmaster and gaining a little glory. 'Well done!' he exclaimed when he saw it, rubbing his hands. 'This is one of the earliest dates for moschatel that I can recollect. Now let me see if I can tell you where you found it.'

My pride began to dwindle into discomfort. 'Could it have been in the green lane leading to Folke?' he asked, 'or near the meeting of the field paths at Tree Island?' I had not the temerity to answer 'Yes' to either of these questions, though I began to see myself close to the jaws of a trap.

'At the bottom of Honeycomb, then?' he persisted.

'N-not quite there, sir,' I stammered.

His blue eyes bore into me. 'Surely not along the stream that flows from there towards the Mill?'

'Yes,' I whispered, awaiting retribution.

There was a desperate pause. 'Well, that's very interesting,' he replied at last. 'Now I come to think of it, I did find it there once, many years ago, but I had quite forgotten. It must have been remarkably well hidden – and, I should say, growing very close to the water.' He paused in reflection, then added: 'Well done! Well done indeed! Now let's write it down: Moschatel – Holt minor.'

I went back to my place feeling that the flower was an absolute trump; and for this reason, as well as for its charming idiosyncracies, I am fond of moschatel and will not admit that it is 'without glory'.

THE DAWN CHORUS

ne of the most beautiful and mysterious of all natural manifestations – performances would perhaps be a better word – is the concerted outburst of song with which birds greet the dawn on Spring and early Summer mornings. It has been called 'The Dawn Chorus', a description which is, I suppose, as apt and brief as could be devised; and it is during May that it produces the greatest volume and variety of sound. I must confess that I have never been good at getting up in the morning, hardly any better now in old age than I was as a boy, but I recall vividly two occasions when I set an alarm clock whose piercing trill should tear my sleep apart well before first light so that I might be up and ready to hear the opening notes.

The first occasion was early in my first summer term at Oxford, and while it was still dark I made my way into Merton College garden and strolled among the trees and along the top of the old city wall waiting for the music to begin. On the second occasion, at Pipers Hill, I did not go into the garden, but leant out of my bedroom window with a note-book in my hand and jotted down the times when each vocalist joined in and the big climaxes were reached. The note-book survived for many years and I append a trancript of my notes. What seems in retrospect a remarkable feature of them is the evidence they give of the number and variety of birds which at that time (the early thirties) inhabited our garden and its immediate surroundings barely twenty miles from Hyde Park Corner. What I cannot be sure of, or recall, is whether the entries correspond with real or 'summer' time, or the exact date, but it must have been mid May. Here is my summary:

4.10 a.m.   cock crowing
4.11   lapwing, snipe 'pikking'
4.15   snipe drumming (outlines of flower beds vaguely discernible)
4.17   partridge, moorhen, snipe drumming, lapwing
4.20   little owl, redshank, snipe drumming

4.21   pheasant, partridge
4.22   turtle dove, cuckoo; others as before
4.24   blackbird (drowsy), mistle-thrush
4.25   robin, hedge-sparrow, redshank again
4.26   song-thrush, lark, greenfinch, wood pigeon
4.27   cuckoo louder (garden lighter and greener)
4.30   glorious blackbirds dominating a maze of sound (colours beginning
        to appear, and I can smell lilac and wallflowers)
4.32   What a chorus!
4.36   wren; persistent cuckoo and blackbirds scolding
4.37   robin, hedge-sparrow noticeable
4.39   willow warbler; so great a maze of sound it is hard to pick out
        individuals
4.40   soaring lark, garden warbler (orange light in sky)
4.41   yaffle, scolding mistle-thrush
4.42   persistent chaffinch and blackbird, wood pigeon
4.47   great tit, great tit, great tit; wren, wood pigeon
4.48   tree pipit; wren, chaffinch, lark, cuckoo
4.51   turtle dove again; great tit, blue tit, tree pipit
4.53   chorus dwindling
4.57   cock crowing; trio – lark, chaffinch, blackbird
5.00   cuckoo again, tree pipit, cock
5.02   solo song-thrush
5.03   little else but thrush, blue tit, distant cuckoo, pheasant
5.10   turtle dove again, song-thrush, close by
5.12   garden warbler again; wren, chaffinch, cuckoo, lark, blue tit
5.15   SILENCE; then the last five noted in quick succession
5.20   lark, willow warbler again and 'pikking' snipe, swooping lapwing
5.25   silence again – except for chirping house-sparrows and a single
        'cuc-koo'.

The chorus I listened to in Merton College garden in 1929 was quite as
Handelian! So deeply, I remember, was I moved by the experience that I
went back to my rooms and wrote a short article about it and boldly sent it
to the Editor of *The Times*, who, to my great delight, accepted it for publica-
tion. An added pleasure was to follow later, for not only was my article
reprinted in a collection of similar pieces under the title 'The Open Air Year',
but in his preface Viscount Grey of Falloden (whose lovely book *The Charm
of Birds* was then and has remained among my 'top ten' on any subject)
singled out my piece for commendation. Bird-lovers will note with a certain
disbelief one surprising contributor to the Merton Chorus, the corncrake. But

I am telling the truth: on many summer mornings from my rooms, which were only a few yards from Christ Church Meadow, I used to hear the bird's strange rasping call. I admit I have not enquired, but I much doubt whether in recent years the corncrake has ventured so far into the city. Indeed I don't think I have heard it anywhere else in the south of England; in the Lake District, yes – and in the Outer Hebrides.

I hope it is not vainglorious if I quote some passages from my article, not only for the description that it gives of that treasured experience long ago in the college garden, but because it indicates that even the undergraduate had begun to perceive how an awareness and response to the beauty of Nature (what other term can I use?) may be regarded as *worship* – just as I felt the birds' wholehearted singing to be. Surely such a paean could not, cannot, be attributed merely to a concourse of impulses to assert territorial rights? Even if a bird's idea of the Creator is even vaguer than mine, it knows Him to be there, somewhere, and acknowledges its duty or its need to praise Him.

This is part of what I wrote:

'There is in the very early morning before dawn a feeling of intent watch-fulness and suspended activity, like that of an animal about to spring; the passive surrender of night is gone, and everything waits in silent prepara-tion for the day. This brooding silence is suddenly broken by the crowing of a cock, the signal for the departure of the spirits of darkness; it is also the herald of the kingdom of day. Its crowing will remain unchallenged perhaps for a quarter of an hour, except for the occasional screech of a lit-tle owl and the distant, drowsy rasp of a corncrake, which sounds as if it were drawing its claws over the teeth of a comb. Then, without a murmur of warning, a spirit seems to move through the garden and before the lis-tener is properly aware the first notes of the chorus have stolen out into the grey, meditative silence. They are sung by the thrushes in the blossom-laden apple-trees, drowsily at first, but gathering in number and volume as the minutes advance. Through them, like drops of molten gold, flow the glorious, mellow phrases of blackbirds, announcing, as it were, the themes of the symphony, until every bush and tree seems to sway in the flood of song and quiver with tremulous rapture.

Soon the tits throw in their curious miscellany of notes – a teasing, chat-tering, tinkling jargon. The cheerful, reiterated cries of the exploring nuthatch penetrate the throng, augmented now by the husky utterance of the greenfinch and the louder and more sustained notes of robins and hedge-sparrows. A brilliant outburst of melody from a wren, like the light of an explosion, brings about a thrilling climax; it gives the lead to the chaffinches, whose joyous treble makes the listener aware of bursting lilacs and drooping yellow laburnums. A cuckoo utters its two clarinet notes, and jackdaws and rooks call out in tones which are incapable of musical representation. So intricate is the maze of sound that it seems impossible that it will ever be unravelled, until a woodpecker tears through it with a peal of derisive laughter.

Despite this ribaldry, the wood pigeons, when the chorus is at its highest, begin making their everlasting pleas, imploring their mates with desperate earnestness to take those two somethings which are never accepted and whose identity will never be ascertained: their passionate cooing fills the whole garden with a drowsy love-sickness which muffles the sharper sounds of the other birds. The chorus begins to dwindle and subside, the different notes going out like candles in the wind, until scarcely more than an hour from the time when it began there is nothing left of its former grandeur but the desultory singing of a few persistent soloists. These are mostly thrushes, unwilling, perhaps, that the only relics of the glorious symphony just ended should be the chatter of sparrows and starlings, pottering about their household duties like garrulous charwomen.

About half an hour still remains before sunrise: a time of expectancy still, yet also of reminiscence, for a marvellous thing has been created and vanished away; the garden is cold and still, but a pool of green seems to have welled up into it and to hold in its depths trees, bushes, grass and flowers like shimmering reflections of themselves. As the minutes slip by and the melodies fade away the listener is forced, even against his will, to admire and wonder at the birds' tribute to the miracle of Creation, and to ponder upon the inability of man, with all his complexity of soul and intellect to achieve with such ease such moments of ecstasy. On some mysterious impulse which drives them all, these small feathered creatures awake, and before eating a morsel of food or following any other pursuit throw their whole vitality and being into the energy of song. In its spontaneous and united expression of joy and happiness the Dawn Chorus is a true thanksgiving for existence, a triumphant vindication of the fundamental beauty of life.

I will end this chapter by asking the reader to go right above my head and bear in mind what Goethe said: 'Certainly there is no more beautiful adoration of the Deity than that which needs no image, that springs up in one's mind merely from intercourse with Nature.'

BOLUS AND BERRIES

ortunate as we were in those far-off, leisured days to have long summer holidays by the sea, sometimes lasting as much as four weeks, it was a joy to be at home again at Pipers Hill for a fortnight or more before the inexorable return to school. Not that I was unhappy at school: far from it, especially when back in the swing of its various activities and companion-ships, its amused and amusing comments on masters and friends, the awakening interests toyed with or doted on, and all those grumbles and crazes; but the transfer from one mode of life to another quite different was always a wrench, nor was it ever anything but disagreeable to exchange the comforts of Home for the rigours of Sparta. (I must interpolate here that punctually on the ante-penultimate day of every term there would arrive from my father a letter or post-card bearing the following jingle: 'To-day's the meat, To-morrow's the bone. The next day after we go home, then [according to the season] hey! for Father Christmas, Easter eggs, or the bay and the beach.' He once missed the post and the first three words of the message came by telegram.)

In the meantime, before we went back to school there were many quiet occupations to enjoy: weeding our small patches of garden by the sand-pit; burying tins of this and that in the sand-pit itself so that they could be dug up as treasure in the Christmas holidays; refurbishing our 'tree-house' in the Wild Patch; trying (in my case) to draw a silvery willow that grew most gracefully on the edge of the Ditch or the solitary oak-tree (the Tree of Life) out in the water-meadows; sorties into the Field, which became a sort of 'spacious firmament' for great moony mushrooms and groups of pearly 'but-tons' like the Pleiades, all as delicious to pluck between second and middle finger as to eat; or just wandering along my mother's herbaceous border to watch the red admirals, the peacocks and small tortoiseshells, the whites, the newly hatched brimstones and the small coppers as they wove their aerial tapestry of colours on wings that added their own rustle to the humming of the bees. And of course there were hilarious games of rounders on the Lawn, boating picnics on the Canal, and expeditions to Wisley and other commons in search of blackberries – Surrey could produce monsters as big as mulberries – and journeys further afield to the North Downs, such as I have described, to look for uncommon butterflies and wild flowers.

But there was one occupation in which my brother and I took particular delight and which is for ever associated in my mind with the Home stretch before the winter term. This was what we called rum-and-treacling and entomologists usually refer to as 'sugaring': in other words, a means of luring moths (poor things!) to be netted or, as time went on, just looked at and admired. As usual my father glamorised the process for us in his inimitable way. He would bring down from his office an odd-shaped parcel impeccably wrapped in paper black rather than brown and bound and knotted in a trellis of white string by one of his clerks (I have never since met with paper quite so dark or string quite so white). With due ceremony he would unwrap a bottle of rum and a tin of black treacle, the treacle to act as lure and the rum as intoxicant; and, calling for a pudding-basin and a wooden spoon, he would pour into the basin first a great coil of treacle, then a splash – or noggin as he called it – of rum and vigorously mix the two with the spoon while licking his lips with a smacking sound that would have been utterly taboo at table. After a pause he would pour in more treacle and more rum until the mixture was truly 'thick and slab' and he thought a sufficient quantity had been made. For the final product, so opulent in texture and smell and of a deep, Rembrandtesque hue, he produced the thrilling, the recondite word Bolus. How eagerly on the appointed day we longed for his return from the City and weather propitious for 'bolusing'! Before supper and while it was still light we would process round the garden ladling out spoonfuls of the bolus onto the trunks of likely trees, notably the almond-tree, with its silky bark, and the oak-trees in the Field, by the Pond and at the White Gate.

We could hardly sit through supper in our impatient wait for darkness to fall. When my father thought the time right we would set out with a net and 'smelling-bottle' and with a torch pointing downward so that the beam could guide our steps but not disturb any moths that might be winging bolus-ward. When we came to each tree we would wait a moment in stillness before my father suddenly lifted his torch so as to reveal how effective the lure had proved. Sometimes, I confess (I still sense our disappointment), there would be little but earwigs, ants or indeterminate beetles; but at others our gaze would fall on a throng of ghostly wings, grey and brown, mottled and streaked and barred, some motionless, some whirring in tipsy delight, and on eyes that glowed like tiny lamps as the torchlight caught them. Many sorts might be there: old ladies, gothics and 'redunders'; cabbages and carpets; arches and angle-shades; tussocks and wainscoats; harts and darts and fig-

ures of eight; copper underwings and broad-bordered yellows; and occasionally the beam would light on the shapely wings of swallow-tails, pale as the 'rathe primrose', and emeralds as green as sea-water flecked with foam. I should like to claim that we saw the whole farrago of prominents, hook-tips, brocades, rustics, characters, snouts and waves, but I cannot; or, if we did, I do not remember them. As for the scarce merveille-du-jour or the lunar double-stripe, I can state positively that neither came our way. I must add here that an old friend of mine, whose knowledge of moths far outstripped my brother's or mine, used to tell me that once upon a time there was a well-known entomologist of Jewish extraction who was known to the fraternity by the name of a small moth of wide distribution, the Setaceous Hebrew Character.

I do not know why moths bring me to berries: doubtless it is because of their association with those bland September days – mild with a tang of latent frost and with the smell of bonfires in the air – before our return to school. Nor am I aware that anyone has written much about them. There ought surely to be a famous set-piece, if not by W.H. Hudson or Edward Thomas, by some eighteenth-century master who would pile up sonorous epithets and phrases in a panegyric worthy of their varied colours and textures, a variety of colours as wide as that of the eggs of wild birds, which have always been a source of wonder and delight to me.

If the robin's treble cadences may be thought of as the theme-song of September, the blackberry should stand for its emblem. The Field was not very productive of blackberries, but at one corner on our side of the lane dividing it from the Rectory paddock, there was a fine tangle of bramble and brier where we once found a long-tailed tit's nest. There we would always find a few sprays of tempting gloss and grandeur, and the scarlet of the innumerable hips complemented the black. The bank a little further along was a good place for 'lords and ladies', whose seed heads held up their crimson embossed truncheons. And further along still, by the gate at the junction of Rectory Lane and the lane to the church there was a stretch of intertwined snowberry and privet: the showers of snowballs on the one and on the other the clusters of glittering black beads were a study in *chiaroscuro*, to which my mind recurs whenever since then I have come upon the same partnership.

Winter brings, as everyone knows, another contrast of a different yet familiar kind when the scarlet of holly berries is set beside the pearly whiteness of the berries of mistletoe, the Golden Bough of mystery and legend. I think of the sprig of holly that was always stuck in the crown of the Christmas pudding and the bunch of mistletoe hanging from the lantern in the hall – with the third of the triumvirate close by, the ivy's fistfuls of berries, each one as black as a match-head topped with a plaque of grey.*

Different in shade and texture from the holly were the berries of the mealy guelder rose that grew by the rubbish heap at the far end of the garden. These, more crimson than scarlet, had for me an almost haunting lustre and translucence. My younger sister, when learning to play the violin, had to go to that remote spot to practise beside them, because the sounds she produced extorted such howls from the dog as the rest of us could not endure; and he would sometimes find her out down there and voice his agony, or ecstasy, we never knew which.

Wherever there were hawthorn hedges round Pipers Hill, they became thick with berries, more matt in texture than were those of the guelder rose, yet achieving in their multitudes the effect of the burning bush that Moses turned aside to see. Out in the water-meadows the elders would become purple with berries, like old-fashioned pin-heads, on stems not steely but red as rubies; the dogwoods held clusters, dark green at first with a touch of 'peacock' before becoming an ever deeper black; and the blackthorn hedge beside the Avenue, where that first thrush's nest sat half hidden by the crowding white blossoms, offered tempting blue sloes, dusted with grey bloom, which, if we dared to taste made our teeth feel as rough as my father's loofah lying on the top of his mighty sponge, at least a foot in diameter, in a big wooden bowl in the bathroom. Beguiling as any were the swathes and swags of bryony, baroque in their exuberance, scarlet when ripe, but at an earlier stage green or yellow, like small balloons. And perhaps most opulent of all I would claim the clusters of rowan berries which used to delight me on a single tree in my Somerset garden, bringing to mind places as far apart in time and distance as the Wild Patch, the mountains of Savoy and the 'banks and braes o' bonny Doon'.

One shrub that we did not find near Home bears berries to which most people, I suppose, would award the prize for combined beauty and quaintness: the spindle, its coral-pink quatrefoil opening to reveal seeds as yellow as egg-yolk – and no bird's egg, despite every modulation of the oval and the pear-shape, can boast a quatrefoil! But in the lanes of Somerset, spindleberries adorn many a hedge as September comes round; and whenever I have found them they seem to sum up the lifelong fascination I have felt for berries, here and there and everywhere, today, yesterday and long ago, at their best when touched by the gentle level sunlight and having for accompaniment the muffled roar of rooks and the yelp of jackdaws as they make their evening flight to the wood over the hill, just as I watched them do in

---

*According to Sir James Frazer's monumental book *The Golden Bough,* the ancient Bacchanals ate ivy 'and their inspired fury was believed to be due to the exciting and intoxicating properties of the plant.'

the old days, in wonder and perplexity at their inscrutable manoeuvres, wayward yet controlled, above the Copse beyond the Field against a lemon-yellow sky.

y mother always referred to and addressed him by his surname, and we children called him 'Gardener'. It was my father, as usual, who invented the characteristic corruption of the two. Jargy (with a hard 'g') was at most seasons of the year a somewhat remote and uncommunicative personage: only during the week before Christmas did he come to the fore, when he sat in the stables which served as his potting shed, and wove his marvellous wreaths.

He lived about a mile away as the crow flies, but quite two miles by road and lane, so that except in the wettest weather he came and went across country – over the Field, through a little copse, along a path bordering the River, and on down a narrow lane over-arched by elms. His cottage was, and perhaps had been, a subject for a Birket Foster watercolour, with its tall chimney-stack and sinuous roof line, its old brickwork and timbering, hardly to be glimpsed in summer for sunflowers and hollyhocks. We would see him in the mornings emerge from the copse by a stile, where in Autumn a bush of guelder rose hung out its clusters of crimson berries and in Summer the tallest yellow flags and purple loosestrife marked the place of my brother's collapse into the Bourne when reaching for a moorhen's nest; and in the evenings we would see him vanish over the stile, just when a kerchief of September mist began to float above the rushes or the clear sunlight of June dissolved in a myriad points of pure colour the flowering meadows.

About a week before Christmas a clip-clipping sound would come from the shrubbery as Jargy gathered the material for his wreaths, and he would be seen wheeling barrow loads of cypress, thuya, laurel and holly towards the stables. There, enthroned on an upturned log, he would set about his task, wearing the green baize apron he always put on for such indoor work as potting seedlings or cleaning knives, and with the cloth cap from which he was almost inseparable slightly tilted back on his grizzled head. From two hooks above his right shoulder hung great masses of bass that made me think with an agreeable shudder of scalps, and since he was a tireless worker the deft weaving of his fingers would be regularly interrupted by the reach of his arm to pull down a fresh strand. Another inseparable companion found him out at lunch time, his robin; and if we could make some excuse to be there at that hour we might be lucky enough to see him unroll a scarlet, white-spotted handkerchief and take out his bread and cheese. There was something magnificent in his total disregard of nursery law as he jabbed a piece of cheese with the blade of his clasp knife and conveyed it direct to his mouth – something most enviable in the impunity of the act.

I reproach myself now for not learning the secret of his craft; perhaps as children we were too much in awe of him to stand beside him too long or ask too many questions. I have often tried to emulate his skill, but the sprays refuse to stay together and loll in dishevelled colpons like the hair of Chaucer's Pardoner. Jargy never used wire; each spray was neatly laid against its neighbour and tied with bass, the pieces being chosen with exquisite taste to blend or contrast their grey-blues, golds and dusky greens. His longest wreath or garland must have been at least fifty feet long, for it started at the foot of the stairs, climbed to the first floor, ran back along the banisters and turned there at right angles to cross the hall above the hooks for the basket swing until it came almost full circle at the front door. The wreaths for the portraits were much shorter – some four feet in length – and were draped across the top to hang down on either side after the fashion of fur stoles upon elegant shoulders.

The garland for the hall was a *tour de force*, but there were two other set pieces. One was the closely woven wreath of variegated holly for the bracket clock on the dining-room mantelpiece, aptly termed by my aunts 'The Judge's Wig'; the other the chaplet of laurel for the circular gilt mirror, surmounted by an eagle, also in the dining-room, which looked down along the table and reflected in its convex glass all that passed there.

The twenty-third of December and the morning of Christmas Eve were dedicated to the putting up of the wreaths. Dust sheets were laid down everywhere; exhortations to keep out of the way or mind where we were treading were as thick in our ears as the berries among the leaves; and Jargy would appear at the front door wrapped in the dark green coils of his handiwork like a new Laocoon. For once he was capless, and it was possible to peer down through the banisters at the snail-like spiral of hair on the crown of his head as he bent to his work. A mysterious resiny fragrance rose from the hall and gradually permeated the house.

When the decorating was all done – when the last picture had been given its coronal, the clock its wig, the mirror its chaplet of laurel and the lantern in the hall its habitual sprig of mistletoe – and when Jargy had cleared away the remnants so that there was not a single berry left to be squashed into the carpet by a careless shoe, he appeared once more on the doorstep, this time to give and receive good wishes for a happy Christmas. There my mother would present him with a tin of tobacco for himself, a packet of tea and some garment for his wife, and a box of crackers for the family. The several packages he tied together with bass and swung over his shoulder and then set off home in the gathering darkness by the footpath way.

The clock now ticks and strikes through the years in my own home. At Christmas it still wears a wig, albeit a travesty of Jargy's – but then I have only a very young bush of variegated holly! If it has the power to listen, as I used to be sure it had since it could speak so plainly, might it not by a stroke of some Dickensian magic one Christmas night repeat a passage from one of those festivals of old? And the mirror, looking down now upon a different table – might we not at the same witching hour chance to find a tiny piece of the rim of its silver mask turned up, allowing us to peal off the whole surface, and then another layer and another, until we came upon the image of one of our Christmas dinner tables of long ago: the candlelight still agleam on glass and mahogany, on the bowls of fruit, the little vase of Christmas roses by my mother's plate and the pyramids of glittering crackers; on the face of the master of the house, still happy and unlined; on that of the mistress also, her hair as yet without a single thread of silver; and in the eyes of the little children that round the table went – all caught and held in miniature within the circle, its circumference fretted by the dark, polished tips of the leaves of Jargy's wreath?

GOLDEN ORIOLE

ery few books gave me more pleasure as a boy than T.A. Coward's *The Birds of the British Isles, their Nests and Eggs* in two volumes. I did not know of the third in the series, dealing with migration, until I was grown up. All three are still in my possession and remain among the books I most often consult. Coward was a master of accurate and, I make bold to say, poetic description; and the illustrations, mainly by Thorburn, a celebrated master of bird portraiture, and an undeservedly neglected artist J.G. Keulmans, have the knack of giving precise expression to the appearance, shape and stance of each bird and placing it in a characteristic setting. So much so that whenever a particular bird is mentioned even today, its portrait in 'Coward', so constantly the object of my boyish scrutiny, returns immediately upon my 'inward eye'.

This is especially true of the pictures of rarities – such as the golden oriole, the cream-coloured courser, Pallas's sand-grouse and the collared pratincole.* Nearly every expedition in search of birds in boyhood and, if the truth be told, in maturer years, has started off in the half-laughing, half-sanguine expectancy of meeting with a collared pratincole. Indeed a youthful ambition was to be the author of a masterpiece entitled *The Collared Pratincole.* Expectation seemed never to be realised – until a few years ago when, in the Camargue, I at last tracked down that nimble and elegant bird bearing a name so delicious to roll round the tongue. But the most resplendent, the most glamorous of all such rarities, continued to be the golden oriole – the name alone works magic – forever perched, as in Coward, with his sober-costumed mate on a fig-tree laden with opulent fruit: could I in reason

---

*Soon after I had grown up I added a fifth: the purple gallinule. And long after that I saw one in Portugal, a dark shape lumbering across a mere with slow wing-beats and legs dangling. A bird-loving friend of mine used to tell me that his lifelong ambition was to see an Andalusian hemipode, but he never got further than hearing a screech in a Spanish marsh which to his dying day he swore was uttered by a native hemipode.

expect to catch sight of such a wonder? Again I was lucky, for that encounter too came to me in time and at the happiest and most fortunate epoch in my life: it was on the day after I had become engaged to be married and the last War was still three months short of a certainty. There was also a most curious sequel which has lodged in my memory.

We had been wandering along a path that wound through a copse of sweet chestnut above Lake Maggiore. We walked in shadow and sunlight beneath the flashing spears of the leaves until the path brought us to a glade deep in grass and flowers. About it grew a palisade of laburnum threaded and looped with golden blossom. We had just sat down beneath a little ash tree, among the narcissi and purple columbines, when a bird's note sounded above our heads – a clear, fluting call in three syllables eagerly repeated. It seemed to be asking a question. At first we could not interpret its message, but in a moment or two we understood. 'How are you?' the bird was calling. 'How are you? How are you?.' There was but one answer and we gave it: 'Happy, happy, happy!' We could see the bird now: its plumage was golden, its wings slashed with black, just as in dear old 'Coward'. The sunlight caught it as it flew between the crowding leaves of the chestnut and the glittering necklaces of laburnum, the lake lying blue beyond.

We asked each other the question and gave the same answer many times during the next day or two, and yet again at the station as the train was about to separate us for a few days, she to remain in Italy and I to return to my office in London. 'Happy?' I exclaimed, mocking her; 'Happy? How can you say that when I am leaving you for ever? Well, isn't a single day away from you an eternity, let alone ten? Promise not to forget. Have you written it down? Friday, the 25th, usual time, usual place. London! It seems a world away. Will the golden oriole be with us there, too?'

The train began to move. 'There, and everywhere, and always,' she called through her tears, mechanically waving her hand.

I found a seat in a carriage with only one occupant, an old woman in black, sprawled in a corner. I did not remark her at first; my mind was too full of the joy the past fortnight had brought. I gazed out half-seeing at the ice-green loops of the river, the clustered villages, the cows that seemed modelled in clay, and the crags with their skeins of silver waterfall.

'You like mountains?' enquired a voice close to me. 'I speak English, for I judge that to be your native tongue. I do not care for them myself. They oppress me. They allow too scant a view of the sky.' I was obliged to say I disagreed; surely one had only to climb them to get all the sky one needed? 'Maybe,' was the reply, 'but I am too old to climb; and struggling as I must along the flat, I am awed by their huge shapes and overpowering presence. Give me the breadth and freedom of the steppes, where I have spent the greater part of my life, or even the little levels of East Anglia, which I can just remember as a child.'

I looked at the shapeless woman in her stained and shabby black dress; at her face the colour of cement; the dry, pallid lips; the huge mole on one cheek, like a shrivelled puff-ball. Was it possible that she had once been a little girl? Or a young woman, glowing and slender, who had known the bewilderment of loving and the ecstasy of being loved, whose happiness had led on to marriage? As if in answer she continued: 'My journey is a sad one – unlike yours, young man, for unless I am mistaken your heart just now has its desire. I am going to Paris to see my son, who is desperately ill. When the hospital wrote to say I must go to him, it seemed out of the question. I had not the money for half the fare. But I am lucky in my boy. Between him and me there is a bond of deep devotion, and I was sure that if only I could sit by his bedside, his hand in mine, with God's help he would get well. And so you see, I *had* to come.'

She paused, and I stammered a few words of sympathy. She looked straight at me. Age and hardship had not ruined her eyes, which were those of Athene, clear as lake water on a grey evening, nor the majestic span of her eyebrows. About her eyes there hovered a smile which did not touch her lips as she said: 'It was my husband who found the money. Fortune has favoured me there too: even after all these years there is nothing he will not do for me. Yet for a White Russian refugee who drives a tumbledown taxi to find the fare from Sofia to Paris – it was a miracle! My other expenses I must cut according to this little purse: I earn what I can by teaching French – and the English I learned long ago in a Norfolk vicarage.'

She paused again, looking out at the darkening valley. 'What day is it?' she asked. 'Monday,' I answered, in some surprise. 'Monday,' she repeated, 'Monday evening! "And the evening and the morning were the third day." I had hoped to be at my son's bedside these twelve hours. I have been sitting here since Saturday afternoon. They told me I should be in Paris on Monday morning, and now I must face a third night in this everlasting train. In the darkness I see my son's haggard face more vividly, and when I doze I dream of it.'

The first service for dinner was announced and, a little ashamed at leaving her, I went along to the dining-car. When I returned to the compartment it was in darkness and she was asleep. I could see by the light in the corridor that her head and shoulders were wrapped in a bright red and green rug and that her lips moved as if she were talking to herself. I had not the heart to turn on the light over my head lest it disturb her. Not that I needed a book to pass the time: my mind had happy occupation enough. Yet my eyes kept returning to the ashen face and the lips now mechanically twitching. They seemed to repeat a brief phrase, in time with the movement of the wheels – a phrase of three beats. The more I looked the stronger the impulse grew to lean forward and catch, if I could, her murmured utterance. But now the train was running into Lausanne and the lights of the city wheeling in through the window disturbed her. The lips became still and she opened her eyes.

At the station a brisk little woman darted into the carriage, snapped on one of the lights and enquired in French if one of the other corner seats was reserved. I replied that it was not and she sat down. She also wore black, but her costume was neat, well pressed and spotless. She had sharp black eyes and a tiny black mole beneath one of them. Everything about her was black: gloves, scarf, shoes, stockings, handbag and suitcase. On her head was a high-crowned, black hat. This she promptly took off, and underneath was a confused mass of grey hair, which was piled up into a little rick fenced about with large tortoiseshell combs. Grasping one of these she dragged it fiercely to and fro, further confounding the confusion, and rammed it back awry. Then she took from her handbag a small black reticule and extracted from it and swallowed a small black pill. Above her head, depending from her suitcase, was a label inscribed in Indian ink – in narrow, gabled characters – 'Madame Citron'. Again I was moved to speculate how marvellously the winds of love, courtship and marriage will blow where they list.

At Vallorbe the French douaniers invaded the carriage, making Madame Citron pay duty on a string of black-skinned sausages. On the old lady from Sofia they levied a crushing impost on a box of Russian cigarettes for her son. Since there was likely to be a long wait, she said she would go in search of some milk, having had no food since morning. She declined my offer to get it for her, but accepted my help in the laborious descent to the platform and lumbered away with a painful heave of the shoulder and dragging of one leg. She was gone for some time and when at last I caught sight of her, it was clear that her errand had been in vain, for she was bending down to drink from the tap in the station wall labelled *Eau potable*.

The night passed uneasily, as nights in the train will. Whereas it seemed almost improper to scrutinise the sleeping countenance of Madame Citron, I found that whenever I was not dozing myself my eyes returned perforce to the face of my other companion. The lips began to twitch more urgently, always to the same rhythm. At length I could resist no longer the impulse to lean forward. I put my face close to hers and caught the words she was muttering: 'How are you? How are you? How are you?'

The morning was sunny. Madame Citron set herself to read half-a-dozen letters thickly edged with black and confided that she was going to the funeral of her unfortunate brother – a topic abruptly changed, with no discernible relevance, to the sculptures in the Louvre. The old lady from Sofia began to enquire anxiously how much she would have to tip her porter and about the price of Paris taxis. As the train drew in to the city I helped her collect her belongings, among them a small bunch of roses for her son which had dwindled in the heat of the long journey to a few papery flakes and brittle stems.

Madame Citron was met by a deputation of relatives in all the panoply of 'Grand Deuil'. Their repeated enquiry – 'Comment allez-vous, chère Célestine?' – floated upon a sea of sobs and ejaculations.

I managed to prevail upon the old lady to let my porter carry her case with mine. I took her arm and felt how little I had done to deserve her outpouring of thanks. I helped her into a taxi and as it gathered speed on its way to the hospital I knew I should not forget the look of apprehension on the pale face at the window; while to the question that seemed now to come involuntarily to her lips I realised with a pang that I should never learn the answer.

When I reached my flat in London that evening I found a telegram from Italy pushed under the door. It contained three words. It was just like her to wire me a golden oriole. How wayward, I reflected solemnly, is the incidence of happiness, and doubtless how fleeting! As a beneficiary of its immediate favour, I could only mutter a short grace – and look forward to Friday, the 25th.

P.S. A year or two after I had written this, my wife and I were the guests of two Hungarian ladies who owned a cottage in a little plot, half garden and half orchard, close to the banks of the great Danube a few miles to the north of Budapest. Luncheon had been laid on trestle tables in the dappled sunlight and shadow of the trees, one of which spread its branches quite low over the delicious and bountiful repast. In an interval of the conversation, which consisted of little else than nods and becks and wreathéd smiles (since the ladies had hardly any English and we no more than a word or two of Hungarian), I happened to look up, and there, hardly four feet above my head, in the fork of a horizontal branch, was a flimsy nest in which a golden oriole was quietly brooding her eggs. And there she remained without moving through all the afternoon, absorbed in her quiet duty.

A WISP OF HAIRSTREAKS

uick, quick!" cried my elder (but then very young) sister in a tone of anguish that caused momentary alarm. 'There's a foreign butterfly here.' Alarm at once gave way to excitement and my brother, flourishing a green net, ran to the spot, I at his heels.

'Where? I bet it isn't,' I exclaimed, though I was the one who was said to imagine things and was called Rider Haggard for the propensity. My sister was standing rigid by a Devonshire blackberry bush in full flower, biting her lips lest her clumsy brothers should put the stranger to flight and hardly daring so much as to point. 'There! It's got tails,' she declared, as if to clinch the matter.

We peered in among the crowded pink and white blossom resonant with the hum of bees and other gauzy-winged insects. There, indeed, sipping nectar and silently wagging its wings, was a strange and lovely butterfly, all brown and orange, scored with black and slashed with silver, and having an undeniable tail on each of the lower wings – not of the length grown by denizens of Assam or the Amazon as seen in picture-books or museums, but even so a tail.

As always on such occasions there was a breathless pause while my brother poised himself for the 'stoop'; the net swept; there was a fluttering of wings beneath the gauze and a moment or two later the treasure was in the killing-bottle. From the standpoint of more philosophic years it is easy to deplore the capture, yet the excitement of the moment was entrancing and unforgettable. And that particular female brown hairstreak (for such it proved to be) for long escaped 'the iniquity of oblivion', surviving at least forty years of move and storage, change and decay, in my brother's cabinet.

The blackberry bush it graced was in a lane near Westward Ho! which ran a little way back from the cliffs beneath the gorse and bracken-covered ridge familiar to readers of *Stalky and Co* as the Fuzzy-Wuzzy. The lane, known locally by the indecorous name of Bumley Scratch, was favoured by butterflies of many kinds, but in all our summer holidays in North Devon – or elsewhere for that matter – we neither caught nor saw another brown hairstreak. Yet the species is said to be widespread through the southern half of the country.

The purple and green hairstreaks we met with more often; and the white-letter hairstreak, inscribed on the underside of each hind wing with a scribbled character – often like a white W or M, depending on the way you look at it – I have seen many times in various southern counties. Indeed, in a valley in south-east Somerset, there was a stretch of hedge close to some fine wych-elms (the leaves of which are the caterpillars' favourite foodstuff), where in early July I could count on seeing five or six of these delightful butterflies; they seemed to prefer the species of bramble that produces pink blossoms, for there were plenty of white-blossoming brambles in the neighbouring hedges where none were to be seen. But this was before the lamentable onset of Dutch elm disease, since when I have looked in vain.

My very first meeting, when I was still at university, with a white-letter hairstreak (does the memory of such encounters ever fade?) was in a little marshy dell in Dorset, full of low-growing brambles and plants like fleabane and watermint, betony and devil's-bit scabious. Again a flowering blackberry bush was host to the new acquaintance; and being older (and in this respect wiser, perhaps) I could watch without wishing to take the small creature as it sipped and sunned itself and showed off the tiny but pronounced points upon the lower wings beneath the bold ripples of orange. The dell was awash with the pungent odour of the watermint, and ever since that day the plant and the butterfly have been linked by the association, each bringing the other to mind.

The gregarious purple hairstreak is much commoner, though local in its preferences. Apart from North Devon, where in the 'twenties it thronged the oaks of favoured glades near Bucks Mills and Clovelly, I connect it – largely for old association's sake – with the beautiful wooded country of the Blackmore Vale. There it showed a partiality for the graceful ash saplings that grew along the edges of the boggy rides through the oakwoods. As schoolboys in Dorset, when our parents came to see us in the latter part of the Summer term, we always asked to be taken to a particular stretch of woodland, and thither in those first years we would fare by horse and carriage.

The weather seems always to have been set fair; the stubborn clay of the rides was baked hard by the July sun and had cracked into treacherous fissures, and in the shimmering heat only the great silver-washed fritillaries that swung and glided in the sunlight on their brilliant cornelian wings showed an effortless activity and only the young ash trees looked cool – cool as

quietly playing fountains. We found that by shaking their thin trunks we
woke the dozing hair-streaks, which would float up and hover, as if they
were wind-blown petals from the tree itself, fluttering on wings that had the
gleam now of grey watered silk, now of black satin shot with purple.

Once, I remember, we went with a party of school friends in a wagonette.
I can see us ranged down either side, in white cricket shorts and round,
floppy grey hats, with a double line of bare knees pressed together; I can feel
the spiny horsehair seats studded with buttons in diamond formation; I can
smell the odour of warm harness and horseflesh; and I can hear the click of
the little door at the back and the creak of the folding steps by which we
climbed in and out. When, in the late afternoon, we had eaten our fill at the
farmhouse which so bountifully restored us near the close of all such expeditions, and had yellowed our noses by too vigorous sniffing at the opulent
tiger lilies in the garden, the two staunch horses and the lumbering vehicle
took us leisurely back through the far-flung shadows and level sunbeams.

Of the rare black hairstreak I cannot speak, since it has never been my fortune to see it alive, but for the green, the most frequent and fairest of the five,
I have an especial affection to be justified in a few moments. A few miles
from Pipers Hill – a little beyond walking distance there and back, but easily attainable on 'bikes' – was a spot known to us as The Impassable Road for
Motors, since there was a notice to that effect at the entrance to the rough
road or lane we were making for. It ran through a delightfully brambly,
brackeny, tussocky stretch, which I believe has now been suffocated by an
airfield. But in my mind's eye it still exists in its original romantic guise, a
splendid place for the beautiful little green hairstreak and, in the summer
holidays, for blackberries and for comma butterflies, which seemed to be
conscious of the harmonious scheme of contrasted colours their flickering,
flame-red wings made with the sumptuous blue of the scabious flowers that
held them in thrall.

It was here that I first saw green hairstreaks: at the end of a Spring holidays which had been prolonged into May because of an epidemic of mumps
in the previous term at school. How capriciously, it may be remarked, can
disagreeable happenings sometimes prepare the way for good! Half-hidden
in a thicket close to The Impassable Road stood the explanation of the
gnarled apple-trees and exuberant lilacs that surprisingly mingled with
bramble and blackthorn – the ruins of a cottage and, at a little distance, a
tumbledown privy darkly hooded with ivy, from which a blackbird fled
squawking, leaving us to enjoy the warmth of her speckled eggs at the tips
of our fingers. The green hairstreaks preferred the lilacs to the apple-trees,
dancing this way and that among the great sweet-smelling cones of purple
blossom.

135

I have called the green hairstreak the fairest of the five because its scheme of colour strikes me as having within that minute compass a perfect simplicity, so bold in contrast between the warm brown of the upper sides of the wings and the radiant green of the under, where the élite of the clan wear across the green as emblem of their name two tiny strings of seed pearls. I think of it particularly in the surroundings I have just described, in the clearings of Kent and Dorset copses, one moment almost invisible against the opening leaves, the next conspicuous among the blue dog violets and yellow pimpernels or flitting between the sea and sky among the scrub of Golden Cap and the other headlands east of Charmouth.

Yet my most cherished association takes me to a glade among the mountains of northern Italy, where the sun shone warm upon the yellow anemones and blue gentians and the wind blew fresh and sparkling from the snows; where in the thickets of birch and hazel and ash the lizards were as green as the hairstreaks' wings; and where in the presence and – as Time has shown – with the blessing of one of these tiny butterflies, I asked the most important question of my life and was granted the answer I desired most to hear.

ANTHOLOGY

ost people, I suppose, unless rooted and grounded in the Puritan ethic, enjoy a modicum of self-indulgence: not a plethora indeed, which plays havoc with both health and temper. But a little of what they fancy . . . ? So I have indulged myself by turning my final chapter into a small anthology of extracts from the work of great writers that bear upon what I have been trying to say and certainly say it much better.

I begin with Wordsworth, who always expresses the highest truths in the briefest form. However familiar, even hackneyed, may be his lines on finding wild daffodils along the shore of Ullswater, they speak to me with grateful insistence as I grow older and discover what a wealth of joy the recollection of some natural beauty can bring when it flashes upon my 'inward eye'. It brings indeed its own sort of poetry, defined in another of his wonderful phrases as 'emotion recollected in tranquility'. I do not intend to include here his daffodil lines, but a quatrain from his great Intimations of Immortality Ode. I quote them because in my old age I give humble and hearty thanks for the ability to remember beautiful sights and sounds that have given me joy.

> *O joy! that in our embers*
> *Is something that doth live,*
> *That Nature yet remembers*
> *What was so fugitive!*

Our 'embers'! The purpose of the word may have been the practical one of providing a rhyme, but how inspired it is! Old age is conscious enough of ashes, but if a glow remains, a light can be kindled.

Wordsworth uses another unexpected word when he speaks of Nature's 'privilege':

> *Through all the years of this our life, to lead*
> *From joy to joy!*

True, indeed, and we are the beneficiaries, as he recalls again and again in his poetry, and nowhere in more exalted language than his 'Lines on Tintern Abbey', all of which I wish I could include here.

I continue with Longfellow, who in many people's judgement, I suppose, said too little in too many words; but every now and then he strikes home, at any rate to me. I have always had a particular affection for his little poem 'The Fiftieth Birthday of Agassiz, May 28th, 1857?' Who on Earth, you may ask, was Agassiz? I have found out: he was a Swiss naturalist, who, among other works, wrote *Contributions to the Natural History of the United States of America* and was an opponent of Darwin's theory of evolution. Here are some of the verses in Longfellow's poem:

> *And Nature, the old nurse, took*
> *The child upon her knee,*
> *Saying: 'Here is a story-book*
> *Thy Father has written for thee'.*
>
> *'Come, wander with me,' she said,*
> *Into regions yet untrod*
> *And read what is still unread*
> *In the manuscripts of God.'*
>
> *And he wandered away and away*
> *With Nature, the dear old nurse,*
> *Who sang to him night and day*
> *The rhymes of the universe*
>
> *And wherever the way seemed long,*
> *Or his heart began to fail,*
> *She would sing a wonderful song,*
> *Or tell a more marvellous tale.*
>
> *So she keeps him still a child*
> *And will not let him go . . .*

As I have said in my foreword, I have *not* gone to regions untrod, nor deciphered any of Nature's unread manuscripts, but wherever my way seemed long or my heart began to fail, I would call to mind the words of a much greater poet, Keats, in lines as famous as Wordsworth's and hardly less hackneyed, the great opening passage of *Endymion:*

> *A thing of beauty is a joy for ever:*
> *Its loveliness increases; it will never*
> *Pass into nothingness; but still will keep*
> *A bower quiet for us, and a sleep*
> *Full of sweet dreams, and health and quiet breathing.*
> *Therefore, on every morrow, are we wreathing*
> *A flowery band to bind us to the earth,*
> *Spite of despondence, of the inhuman dearth*
> *Of noble natures, of the gloomy days,*
> *Of all the unhealthy and o'er-darkened ways*
> *Made for our searching: yes, in spite of all,*
> *Some shape of beauty moves away the pall*
> *From our dark spirits. Such the sun, the moon,*
> *Trees old and young, sprouting a shady boon*
> *For simple sheep; and such are daffodils*
> *With the green world they live in . . .*

Phrase after phrase chimes with my own feelings and experience. I think of my father, whose life's work collapsed in his early sixties, leading through o'er-darkened ways to his death and the break-up of our home. I also think of certain years in my own life when my work failed me – or perhaps I failed it – and I fell into moods of despondency from which I barely escaped. How often, *in spite of all*, some shape of beauty moved away the pall from his and my dark spirits! And though Fate was far kinder to me than to him there were times then, and have been since, when something akin to daffodils and the green world they live in have supplied me with the quiet bower I needed.

I will bring in here a sentence on a similar theme from Hazlitt that has always pleased me. In his essay 'On the Love of the Country' he speaks with eloquence about the associations of natural objects with our childhood and the permanence of our attachment to them, whether it be 'the cool shadow of a tree or the sound of a brook running at its feet'; and he sums it up thus:

> For him, then, who has well acquainted himself with Nature's works, she wears always one face, and speaks the same well-known language, striking on the heart, amidst unquiet thoughts, and the tumult of the world, like the music of one's own tongue heard in some far-off country.

Hazlitt, it will be remembered, passed his days in some turbulence, but is

139

said to have ended them with the dying assertion, 'I have led a happy life.' It is clear that the contemplation of Nature's works helped him to that conclusion.

I do not recall what opinion Hazlitt had of Doctor Johnson: I hope the step from one to the other is not too much of a leap. Readers of my book will have noticed that I have tried to show my own love of natural objects and say something in praise of their Creator by portraying some of the smaller of His works as best I can in my drawings. This particular attempt has brought me almost as much pleasure as the general observation of them, since I have been obliged to take a very close look at their exquisite shapes and patterns. Plants, for instance, when in growth, in flower, or in fruit show a striking array of solid forms, small though they may be, and linear designs of infinite variety, small in compass though they are too. The Almighty is surely the best of all designers! So my liking for this short statement by the great Doctor will be understood:

There is nothing, so little for so little a creature as man. It is by studying little things that we attain the great art of having as little misery and as much happiness as possible.

It would be salutary, I think, if this observation were placed above the entrance to every school, so great is the reward of studying little things. And it will be remembered that Blake could see a world in a grain of sand and Heaven in a wild flower.

My love of drawing, however imperfect my skill in it, has through all my life accompanied a love of pictures. (My love of poetry is perhaps self evident.) I have tried, so far as circumstances and my income have allowed, to see as many as I could of the masterpieces of European painting and drawing: I insist upon drawing, because it is the drawings that I have loved most. Music also has given me uncounted hours of pleasure, despite my lamentable ignorance of how it is made; its 'science' I suppose is the term I should use. Yet for all this, I have to admit being in Landor's company when he said 'Nature I loved and, next to Nature, Art,' Nature gaining the priority. So I was delighted some years ago to find, in a somewhat unexpected source, the following passage in Chapter XI of *Mansfield Park:*

Fanny spoke her feelings. 'Here's harmony!' said she. 'Here's repose! Here's what may leave all painting and music behind, and what poetry can only attempt to describe. Here's what may tranquillize every care, and lift the heart to rapture! When I look out on such a night as this, I feel as if there could be neither wickedness nor sorrow in the world; and there cer-

tainly would be less of both if the sublimity of Nature were more attend-
ed to, and people were carried more out of themselves by contemplating
such a scene.'

'I like to hear your enthusiasm, Fanny,' [said Edmund]. 'It is a lovely night,
and they are much to be pitied who have not been taught to feel in some
degree as you do – who have not at least been given a taste for nature
early in life. They lose a great deal.'

'*You* taught me to think and feel on the subject, cousin.'

The man, apart from my father, who taught me to think and feel on the
subject was the Headmaster of my preparatory school, Littleton Powys,
brother of the celebrated writers; so I make no apology for including here
some passages he drew my attention to, with certain comments of his own.
He sent me once in a letter the following translation from the Greek of one
of the 'Sayings of Jesus' in the Oxyrrhynchus papyri, discovered by Grenfell
and Hunt at the beginning of the present century:

Jesus saith: 'Ye ask? Who are those that draw us to the Kingdom, if the
Kingdom is in Heaven? . . . The fowls of the air, and all beasts that are
under the earth and upon the earth, and the fishes of the sea; these are
they that draw you, and the Kingdom is within you.'

Littleton added: 'So in our pursuits of a knowledge of Nature and our love of
it we are carrying out Jesus's advice and sometimes do find glimpses of the
Kingdom of Heaven which is within us.' And in one of his last letters to me
– our correspondence covered almost thirty years until his death in 1955 – he
wrote on the subject of Education: 'I know that Natural History is the most
important subject. There is always something at your doorstep to which you
may go for moral help and strength.' Here is another maxim for the attention
of our schools, and how heartily, towards the end of my life, I endorse it!

He would have reproached me with a laugh for what he would have
termed arrogance in my linking him with Goethe, yet in the closing years of
his life he loved reading 'Goethe's Conversations with Eckermann', and
quoted to me more than once the great philosopher poet's declaration (I
have quoted it in a previous chapter): 'Certainly there is no more beautiful
adoration of the Deity than that which needs no image, that springs up in
one's mind merely from intercourse with Nature.' Yet speaking for Littleton
as well as myself, we both needed the visible and tangible images to assist
adoration!

As I approach the end of my small anthology, I should like to repeat the
theme touched on at the beginning. Now that I am as old as I am, I often

experience a sense of wonderment that I am still alive – that the embers still have a glow in them! I read somewhere recently the following passage from the Sanskrit epic *Mahabharata*, compiled during the four centuries surrounding the life of Christ and thought it apposite:

And what is the greatest marvel? Each day death strikes and we live as though we were immortal. That is what is the greatest marvel!

It is a marvel I try to be constantly thankful for.

My last extract, a poem by the most exquisite of our century's poets, Walter de la Mare, says everything I have been trying to say and, in voicing a wish of mine, something more:

FARE WELL

When I lie where shades of darkness
Shall no more assail mine eyes,
Nor the rain make lamentation
When the wind sighs:
How will fare the world whose wonder
Was the very proof of me?
Memory fades, must the remembered
Perishing be?

O when this my dust surrenders
Hand, foot, lip, to dust again,
May these loved and loving faces,
Please other men!
May the rusting harvest hedgerow
Still the Traveller's joy entwine
And as happy children gather
Posies once mine.

Look thy last on all things lovely
Every hour. Let no night
Seal thy sense in deathly slumber
Till to delight
Thou have paid thy utmost blessing;
Since that all things thou wouldst praise
Beauty took from those who loved them
In other days.

142

POSTSCRIPT

Some years ago the water-meadows I have described in these pages were drained and listened no longer to the call of lapwing and redshank and the drumming of the snipe. Now a motor-way roars past Pipers Hill, tearing apart meadow and garden: and the house, so I hear, stands bowed beside it, a wreck. Something of what it all was and has been in memory, I have tried to set down in these pages. What it is, I dare not bring myself to go and see.

Can it be that joy and happiness and, if you will, beauty, being themselves insubstantial, are not destroyed when material things, including our corporal frame, perish? I call to my aid the fifteenth chapter of St Paul's first epistle to the Corinthians, fondly trusting that the happiness and joy we have found or created, even the phase of existence they blessed, will also have put on immortality and be found in that new dimension which faith and hope encourage us to believe we may one day enter.

And here I should like to add some more lines of verse, long loved, from Dryden's paraphrase of the Twenty-ninth Ode of the Third Book of Horace:

> *Be fair, or foul, or rain, or shine,*
> *The joys I have possest, in spight of fate, are mine.*
> *Not Heaven itself upon the past has pow'r;*
> *But what has been, has been, and I have had my hour.*